Praise for P. D. JAMES'S

Talking About Detective Fiction

"[P. D. James's] literary sensibility—calm observation and exact description—is on ample display here." —*The Wall Street Journal*

"An avid book-length essay on the roots, ethics and methods of the detective story. . . . Her opinions are often surprising and determinedly contrary. . . . Refreshingly outspoken." —*The New York Times*

"An amiable, personal appreciation of the genre by someone who has been one of its most accomplished and popular exponents." —*The Times* (London)

"It's like sitting across from P. D. James over tea, and that, naturally, is a delight." —*Booklist*

"Anyone who is interested in P. D. James's own fiction will want to read this, but it stands in its own right as a deeper, more thoughtful enquiry into what it is we get out of detective fiction. . . . Elegant and thoughtful." —*The Independent* (London)

P. D. JAMES

Talking About Detective Fiction

P. D. James is the author of twenty previous books, most of which have been filmed and broadcast on television in the United States and other countries. She spent thirty years in various departments of the British Civil Service, including the Police and Criminal Law Departments of Great Britain's Home Office. She has served as a magistrate and as a governor of the BBC. In 2000 she celebrated her eightieth birthday and published her autobiography, *Time to Be in Earnest*. The recipient of many prizes and honors, she was created Baroness James of Holland Park in 1991 and was inducted into the International Crime Writing Hall of Fame in 2008. She lives in London and Oxford.

P. D. James

Talking About Detective Fiction

Vintage Books
A Division of Random House, Inc.
New York

FIRST VINTAGE BOOKS EDITION, MAY 2011

Copyright © 2009 by P. D. James

All rights reserved. Published in the United States by Vintage Books,
a division of Random House, Inc., New York, and in Canada by
Random House of Canada Limited, Toronto. Originally published in
hardcover in Great Britain by the Bodleian Library, and subsequently
published in hardcover in the United States by Alfred A. Knopf,
a division of Random House, Inc., New York, in 2010.

Vintage and colophon are registered trademarks of Random House, Inc.

Cartoons used in Foreword, Chapters 4, 5, and 6:
www.CartoonStock.com. Cartoons used in Chapters 1, 2, and 8:
reproduced with permission of Punch Ltd., www.punch.co.uk.
Cartoon used in Chapter 3: from author's own collection.
Cartoon used in Chapter 7: David Brown/artizans.com.

The Library of Congress has cataloged the Knopf edition as follows:
James, P. D.
Talking about detective fiction / by P. D. James.—1st American ed.
p. cm.
1. Detective and mystery stories, English—History and criticism.
I. Title.
PR830.D4J36 2009
823'.8—dc22
2009038501

Vintage ISBN: 978-0-307-74313-8

Book design by Virginia Tan

www.vintagebooks.com

Printed in the United States of America
10 9 8 7 6 5 4 3 2 1

Contents

v

It's a blood curdling novel about the brutal murder of a publisher who rejected a book about the brutal murder of a publisher . . .

Foreword

THIS BOOK had its beginnings in December 2006, when, at the request of the Bodleian's Publishing Department, the then Librarian invited me to write a book on British detective fiction in aid of the Library. As a native of Oxford I had known from early childhood that the Bodleian Library is one of the oldest and most distinguished in the world, and I replied that I was very happy to accept the invitation but must first finish the novel on which I was then working. The book which I was privileged to write now makes its somewhat belated appearance. I was relieved that the subject proposed was one of the few on which I felt competent to pontificate, but I hope that the many references to my own methods of working won't be seen as hubris; they are an attempt to answer some of the questions most frequently asked by my readers and are unlikely to be new to audiences who have heard me speaking about my work over the years—nor, of course, to my fellow crime-writers.

Because of its resilience and popularity, detective fiction has attracted what some may feel is more than its fair share of critical attention, and I have no wish to add to, and less to emulate, the many distinguished studies of the last two centuries. Inevitably there will be some notable omissions, for which I apologise, but my hope is that this short personal account will interest and entertain not only my readers, but the many who share our pleasure in a form of popular literature which for over fifty years has fascinated and engaged me as a writer.

P. D. James

Talking About
Detective Fiction

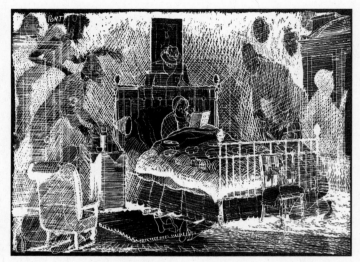

THE BRITISH CHARACTER.
Love of detective fiction.

I

What Are We Talking About and How Did It All Begin?

Death in particular seems to provide the minds of the Anglo-Saxon race with a greater fund of innocent amusement than any other single subject.

Dorothy L. Sayers

THESE WORDS were written by Dorothy L. Sayers in her preface to a volume entitled *Great Short Stories of Detection, Mystery and Horror, Third Series*, published by Gollancz in 1934. She was, of course, talking not of the devastating amalgamation of hatred, violence, tragedy and grief which is real-life murder, but of the ingenious and increasingly popular stories of mystery and detection of which, by that time, she herself was an established and highly regarded writer. And to judge by the worldwide success of Arthur Conan Doyle's Sherlock Holmes and Agatha Christie's Poirot, it is not only the Anglo-Saxons who have an appetite for mystery and mayhem. It seems that this vicarious enjoyment in "murder considered as a fine art," to quote Thomas De Quincey, makes the whole world kin.

In his book *Aspects of the Novel*, E. M. Forster writes:

> "The king died and then the queen died" is a story. "The king died, and then the queen died of grief" is a plot. . . . "The queen died, no one knew why, until it was discovered that it was through grief at the death of the king." This is a plot with a mystery in it, a form capable of high development.

To that I would add, "Everyone thought that the queen had died of grief until they discovered the puncture mark in her throat." That is a murder mystery, and it too is capable of high development.

Novels which enshrine a mystery, often involving a crime, and which provide the satisfaction of an ultimate solution are, of course, common in the canon of English literature, and most would never be thought of in terms of detective fiction. Anthony Trollope, who, like his friend Dickens, was fascinated by the criminal underworld and the exploits of the newly formed detective force, frequently teases us in his novels with a central mystery. Did Lady Eustace steal the family diamonds, and if not, who did? Did Lady Mason forge the codicil to her husband's will in *Orley Farm*, a codicil from which she and her son had benefited for thirty years? Perhaps Trollope gets closest to the conventions of the orthodox detective story in *Phineas Redux*, in which the hero is arrested for the murder of his political enemy, Mr. Bonteen, and only escapes conviction on strong circumstantial evidence by the energetic efforts of Madame Max, the woman who loves him and obtains the vital clue which helps to convict the true murderer. Who is the mysterious woman in white in Wilkie Collins's novel of that name? In Charlotte Brontë's *Jane Eyre*, who is it that Jane hears shrieking in the night, who attacks the mysterious visitor to Thornfield Hall, and what part does the servant Grace Poole play in these dark matters? Charles Dickens provides both mystery and murder in *Bleak House*, creating in Inspector Bucket one of literature's most memorable detectives, while his unfinished novel *The Mystery of Edwin Drood* contains enough of the plot to encourage fascinating conjecture about how it was to be resolved.

A modern example of a novel which enshrines a mystery and its solution is John le Carré's *Tinker, Tailor, Soldier, Spy*. This is generally regarded as one of the most distinguished modern novels of espionage, but it is also a perfectly constructed detective story. Here the central mystery is not an act of murder but the identity of the mole at the heart of the British Secret Service. We know the names of the five suspects, and the setting gives us access to a secret esoteric and cloistered world, making us privileged participants in its mysteries. The detective called in to identify the traitor is John le Carré's sympathetic serial hero George Smiley, with the help of his junior colleague Peter Guillam, and the solution at the end of the novel is one which we the readers should be able to arrive at from evidence fairly presented.

But perhaps the most interesting example of a mainstream novel which is also a detective story is the brilliantly structured *Emma* by Jane Austen. Here the secret which is the mainspring of the action is the unrecognised relationships between the limited number of characters. The story is confined to a closed society in a rural setting, which was to become common in detective fiction, and Jane Austen deceives us with cleverly constructed clues (eight immediately come to mind)—some based on action, some on apparently innocuous conversations, some in her authorial voice. At the end, when all becomes plain and the characters are at last united with their right partners, we wonder how we could have been so deceived.

So what exactly are we talking about when we use the words "detective story," how does it differ from both the mainstream novel and crime fiction, and how did it all begin? Novels which have an atrocious crime at their heart, whose writers set out to explore and interpret the dangerous and violent underworld of crime, its causes, ramifications and effect on both perpetrators and victims, can cover an extraordinarily broad spectrum of imaginative writing extending to some of the highest works of the human imagination. These books may indeed have murder at their heart, but there is frequently no mystery about the perpetrator and therefore no detective and no clues. An example is Graham Greene's *Brighton Rock*. We know from the beginning that Pinkie is a killer and that the unfortunate Hale, desperately walking the streets and lanes of Brighton, knows, as do we, that he is going to be murdered. Our interest is not primarily in the investigation of murder, but in the tragic fate of those involved.

The novel adumbrates Greene's preoccupation with the moral ambiguity of evil, which is at the heart of his creativity; indeed, he came to regret the detective element in *Brighton Rock* and his own division of his novels between "entertainments" and those presumably which he intended should be taken seriously. I'm glad that Greene later repudiated this puzzling dichotomy, which picked out certain of his novels for disparagement and which helped to promote the still prevalent habit of dividing novels into those which are popular, exciting and accessible but, perhaps for these reasons, tend to be undervalued, and those in a somewhat ill-defined category which are granted the distinction of being described as literary novels. Greene surely couldn't have meant that, when writing an "entertainment," he took less trouble with the literary style, cared less for the truth of characterisation and modified the plot and theme to accommodate what he saw as the popular taste. This is manifestly not true of a writer of whom the words of Robert Browning are particularly appropriate:

Our interest's on the dangerous edge of things.
The honest thief, the tender murderer,
The superstitious atheist.

Although the detective story at its highest can also operate on the dangerous edge of things, it is differentiated both from mainstream fiction and from the generality of crime novels by a highly organised structure and recognised conventions. What we can expect is a central mysterious crime, usually murder; a closed circle of suspects, each with motive, means and opportunity for the crime; a detective, either amateur or professional, who comes in like an avenging deity to solve it; and, by the end of the book, a solution which the reader should be able to arrive at by logical deduction from clues inserted in the novel with deceptive cunning but essential fairness. This is the definition I have usually given when speaking about my work but, although not inaccurate, it now seems unduly restrictive and more appropriate to the so-called Golden Age between the wars than it is today. Not all the villains are among a small group of obvious suspects; the detective may be faced with a single named or secret adversary who must be finally run down and defeated by logical deduction from observed facts and, of course, by the accepted heroic virtues: intelligence, courage and energy. This type of mystery is frequently a highly personal conflict between the hero and his prey, characterised by physicality, ruthlessness and violence, often amounting to torture, and even if the detective element is strong, the book is more appropriately described as a thriller than a detective story. The James Bond novels of Ian Fleming are the obvious example. But for a book to be described as detective fiction there must be a central mystery, and one that by the end of the book is solved satisfactorily and logically, not by good luck or intuition, but by intelligent deduction from clues honestly if deceptively presented.

One of the criticisms of the detective story is that this imposed pattern is mere formula writing, that it binds the novelist in a straitjacket which is inimical to the artistic freedom which is essential to creativity, and that subtlety of characterisation, a setting which comes alive for the reader and even credibility are sacrificed to the dominance of structure and plot. But what I find fascinating is the extraordinary variety of books and writers which this so-called formula has been able to accommodate, and how many authors have found the constraints and conventions of the detective story liberating rather than inhibiting of their creative imagination. To say that one cannot produce a good novel within the discipline of a formal structure is as foolish as to say that no sonnet can be great poetry since a sonnet is restricted to fourteen lines—an octave and a sestet—and a strict rhyming sequence. And detective stories are not the only novels which conform to a recognised convention and structure. All Jane Austen's novels have a common storyline: an attractive and virtuous young woman surmounts difficulties to achieve marriage to the man of her choice. This is the age-long convention of the romantic novel, but with Jane Austen what we have is Mills & Boon written by a genius.

And why murder? The central mystery of a detective story need not indeed involve a violent death, but murder remains the unique crime and it carries an atavistic weight of repugnance, fascination and fear. Readers are likely to remain more interested in which of Aunt Ellie's heirs laced her nightly cocoa with arsenic than in who stole her diamond necklace while she was safely holidaying in Bournemouth. Dorothy L. Sayers's *Gaudy Night* doesn't contain a murder, although there is an attempt at one, and the death at the heart of Frances Fyfield's *Blood from Stone* is a spectacular and mysterious suicide. But, except in those novels of espionage which are primarily concerned with treachery, it remains rare for the central crime in an orthodox mystery to be other than the ultimate crime for which no human reparation can ever be made.

So how and when did detective fiction become an accepted genre of popular fiction? To this there is no easy or generally accepted answer. The novel itself is a comparatively recent product of the human imagination, hence its name. It cannot, for example, match the ancient lineage of drama and, unlike drama and verbal storytelling, it can appeal to only a privileged minority until a community achieves a high level of literacy. Storytelling is, of course, an ancient art. Tales which combine excitement with mystery, which offer a puzzle and a solution, can be found in ancient literature and legend and were probably told even earlier by the tribal storyteller round the camp fires of our remote ancestors. Their tales were surely more likely to have dealt with heroic action, revenge and mystery than with subtle ambiguities of character and the domestic problems of the warring couple in the next cave. And novels were being written and read for decades before readers, publishers, critics and booksellers thought of defining them in such categories as Mystery, Thriller, Romantic Fiction, Fantasy or Science Fiction, divisions which are often more a matter of convenience, marketing strategy, taste or prejudice than of fact, and which can be unhelpful to both the novels and their writers.

Some historians of the genre claim that the detective story proper, which fundamentally is concerned with the bringing of order out of disorder and the restoration of peace after the destructive eruption of murder, could not exist until society had an official detective force, which in England would be in 1842, when the detective department of the Metropolitan Police came into being. A distinguished detective novelist, Reginald Hill, creator of the Yorkshire duo Andrew Dalziel and Peter Pascoe, wrote in 1978, "Let me be clear. Without a police force there can be no detective fiction although several modern writers have, with varying degrees of success, tried to write detective stories set in pre-police days." This opinion seems rational: detective fiction is unlikely to flourish in societies without an organised system of law enforcement or in which murder is commonplace. Mystery novelists, particularly in the Golden Age, were generally strong supporters of institutional law and order, and of the police. Individual officers might be portrayed as ineffective, plodding, slow-witted and ill-educated, but never as corrupt. Detective fiction is in the tradition of the English novel, which sees crime, violence and social chaos as an aberration, virtue and good order as the norm for which all reasonable people strive, and which confirms our belief, despite some evidence to the contrary, that we live in a rational, comprehensible and moral universe. And in doing this it provides not only the satisfaction of all popular literature, the mild intellectual challenge of a puzzle, excitement, confirmation of our cherished beliefs in goodness and order, but also entry to a familiar and reassuring world in which we are both involved in violent death and yet remain personally inviolate both from responsibility and from its terrors. Whether we should expect this detachment from vicarious responsibility is, of course, another question and one which bears on the difference between the books of the years between the wars and the detective novels of today.

One strand of the tangled skein of detective fiction goes back to the eighteenth century and includes the gothic tales of horror written by Ann Radcliffe and Matthew "Monk" Lewis. Those gothic novelists were chiefly concerned to enthral readers with tales of terror and the horrific plight of the heroine, and although these books embodied puzzles and riddles, they were concerned far more with horror than with mystery. We recall the scene in Jane Austen's *Northanger Abbey* where the heroine, Catherine Morland, and her friend Isabella meet to discuss their current reading. Isabella says:

> "I will read you their names directly; here they are, in my pocket-book. Castle of Wolfenbach, Clermont, Mysterious Warnings, Necromancer of the Black Forest, Midnight Bell, Orphan of the Rhine, and Horrid Mysteries. Those will last us some time."
>
> "Yes, pretty well; but are they all horrid, are you sure they are all horrid?"

They were indeed, but since the detective story deals with rational terror, their influence on the later development of the genre has been limited, although there are echoes of half-supernatural terror in some of Conan Doyle's stories. Some critics might argue that horror plays a far greater part than ratiocination in the modern psychological mysteries which deal primarily with atrocious serial murders by psychopaths. The most effective are those by writers with personal involvement in the investigation of serial murder, the Americans Patricia Cornwell and Kathy Reichs and, in this country, Val McDermid, whose central character, Tony Hill, is a psychological profiler, and whose novels show evidence of the careful research necessary both for mood and for credibility. These novels, which are becoming increasingly popular, could be said to constitute a separate genre in crime fiction as they do in films.

If we are looking for the origins of detective fiction, most critics are agreed that the two novelists who vie for the distinction of writing the first full-length classical detective story are William Godwin, Shelley's father-in-law, who in 1794 published *Caleb Williams*, and Wilkie Collins, whose best-known novel, *The Moonstone*, appeared in 1868. Neither writer would have been gratified at this posthumous distinction. Wilkie Collins in particular saw himself as a mainstream novelist, albeit one who worked within the category which Victorians described as sensational. These works of mystery, suspense and danger with an overlay of horror had an increasingly strong hold on the popular imagination, and there was much argument among critics, both about their literary merit and about their social desirability. Did these sensational outpourings even deserve the name of novel, or were they a new and inferior form of fiction provided to meet a rapacious public demand focused on W. H. Smith railway station bookstalls? This debate has, of course, continued, but in the mid-nineteenth century it was a new and particular concern. In 1851 *The Times* complained:

> Every addition to the stock [of the bookstalls] was positively made on the assumption that persons of the better class who constitute the larger portion of railway readers lose their accustomed taste the moment they enter the station.

In 1863 a leading review in the *Quarterly Review* stated:

> A class of literature has grown up around us . . . playing no inconsiderable part in moulding the minds and forming the habits and tastes of its generation; and doing so principally, we had almost said exclusively, by "preaching to the nerves." . . . Excitement, and excitement alone, seems to be the great end at which they aim. . . . Various causes have been at work to produce this phenomenon of our literature. Three principal ones may be

named as having had a large share in it—
periodicals, circulating libraries, and railway bookstalls.

By 1880 Matthew Arnold was describing these
novels as "cheap . . . hideous and ignoble of
aspect . . . tawdry novels which flare in the book-
shelves of our railway stations, and which seem
designed, as so much else that is produced for the
use of our middle-class, for people with a low
standard of life." The unfortunate Mr. W. H.
Smith, whose bookstalls did so much to promote
reading, had apparently much to answer for.

But in my view the final and accurate words
about the controversy were written by Anthony
Trollope in his *Autobiography*, published posthumously in 1883.

A good novel should be both [realistic
and sensational], and both in the highest
degree. . . . Truth let there be—truth of
description, truth of character, human
truth as to men and women. If there be
such truth, I do not know that a novel can
be too sensational.

Trollope was undoubtedly categorised by his contemporaries as a sensational novelist and was here

defending his own work, but these words are as true of the sensational novel of today as they were when they were written.

Both *Caleb Williams* and *The Moonstone* could be described as sensational. Hazlitt, the theatre critic and essayist (1778–1830), thought that nobody who began *Caleb Williams* could fail to finish it and that nobody who read it could possibly forget it, yet I have to admit that in adolescence I found it difficult to get through and now have only the vaguest memory of its long and complicated plot. Certainly the novel has at its heart a murder, an amateur detective—Caleb Williams—who tells the story, a pursuit, disguise, clues to the truth of the murder for which two innocent men were hanged, and at the end a deathbed confession. But Godwin was using this dramatic and complicated adventure story to promote his belief in an ideal anarchism and, so far from justifying the rule of law, *Caleb Williams* was intended to show that to trust in social institutions is to invite betrayal. The novel is important both to English fiction generally and to the history of the detective story because Godwin was the first writer to use what he hoped would be a popular form as propaganda on behalf of the poor and exploited, and in particular to expose the injustice of the legal system. This was not a path followed by writers of the interwar years, who were more interested in puzzling and entertaining their readers than in the defects of contemporary society, and I would argue that, with a very few exceptions, it is mainly the modern detective writers who have set out not only to provide an exciting and credible mystery, but to examine and criticise the world which their characters inhabit. Today, however, this is done with less didacticism and more detachment and subtlety than was shown by William Godwin, and arises from the reality of the characters and their world rather than from any ostensible desire to promote a particular social doctrine.

But if one is to award the distinction of being the first detective story to one single novel, my choice—and I think the choice of many others—would be *The Moonstone*, which T. S. Eliot described as "the first, the longest and the best" of modern English detective novels. In my view no other single novel of its type more clearly adumbrates what were to become the main characteristics of the genre. The Moonstone is a diamond stolen from an Indian shrine by Colonel John Herncastle, left to his niece Rachel Verrinder and brought to her Yorkshire home to be handed over on her eighteenth birthday by a young solicitor,

Franklin Blake. During the night it is stolen, obviously by a member of the household. A London detective, Sergeant Cuff, is called in, but later Franklin Blake takes over the investigation, although he himself is among the suspects. *The Moonstone* is a complex and brilliantly structured story told in narrative by the different characters involved directly or indirectly in the story. The varied styles, voices and viewpoints not only add variety and interest to the narrative, but are a powerful revelation of character.

Collins is meticulously accurate in his treatment of medical and forensic details. There is an emphasis on the importance of physical clues—a bloodstained nightdress, a smeared door, a metal chain—and all the clues are made available to the reader, foreshadowing the tradition of the fair-play rule whereby the detective must never be in possession of more information than the reader. The clever shifting of suspicion from one character to another is done with great adroitness, and this emphasis on physical evidence and the cunning manipulation of the reader were both to become common in succeeding mysteries. But the novel has other and more important virtues as a detective story. Wilkie Collins is excellent at describing the physical appearance and the

atmosphere of the setting, particularly the contrast between the secure and prosperous Victorian Verrinder household and the eerie loneliness
of the shivering sands; between the exotic and
accursed jewel that has been stolen and the out-
wardly respectable privileged lives of upper-class
Victorians. The novel provides an interesting
insight into many aspects of its age, particularly
through the truth and variety of its characterisation, and since clue-making is largely concerned
with the minutiae of everyday life, this reflection
of contemporary social mores was to become one
of the most interesting features of the detective
story. The innovative importance of *The Moonstone* was recognised at the time. Henry James
acknowledged its influence in an article in *The
Nation.*

To Mr. Collins belongs the credit of having
introduced into fiction those most mysterious of mysteries, the mysteries which are
at our own doors. This innovation . . . was
fatal to the authority of Mrs. Radcliffe and
her everlasting castle in the Apennines.
What are the Apennines to us or we to
the Apennines? Instead of the terrors of
"Udolpho," we were treated to the terrors

of the cheerful country-house and the busy London lodgings.

Wilkie Collins was innovative in more than the setting. In the rose-growing detective Sergeant Cuff, Wilkie Collins created one of the earliest professional detectives, eccentric but believable, shrewdly knowledgeable about human nature and based on a real-life Scotland Yard inspector, Jonathan Whicher. *The Moonstone* is the only detective novel as far as I know in which the hero is so obviously based on a real-life police officer; the case to which he was summoned to investigate, the murder at Road Hill House in Wiltshire, caused a country-wide sensation at the time and became one of the most intriguing and written-about murders of the nineteenth century. The year was 1860, the place was the detached, impressive home of a prosperous factory inspector, Samuel Kent, and his second wife, Mary, and the victim, their three-year-old son, Francis Saville. On the night of 29 June he was taken from his cot in the room next to the marital bedroom, and carried from the house while the family and servants slept. His body with its throat slashed was found next morning in a privy in the garden. There could be no doubt that the killer was either a member of the family or one of the domestic staff, and the atmosphere of fascinated horror and conjecture spread from the neighbourhood to the whole country, while the local police tried to cope with a crime which, from the first, proved well beyond their powers.

In June 1842 the Home Office had approved the setting up of an elite detective force to investigate particularly atrocious crimes, and Whicher was its most famous and successful member, lauded by Dickens, friend of the famous and something of a national hero. When the local police proved ineffective, Whicher was called in to take over the investigation. The horror of the deed, the age and innocence of the victim, the prosperous upper-class setting, the rumours of sexual scandal and the near certainty that the murderer was one of the household provoked a nationwide heady mixture of revulsion and fascination. It seemed that the whole country, uninhibited by considerations of family grief or privacy, was composed of amateur detectives both in the press and in personal gossip. Whicher was convinced from the start that Constance, the sixteen-year-old half-sister of the child, was guilty, but the arrest of the daughter of a respectable upper-class family provoked outrage. When Constance was released by the magistrates and the case remained unsolved, Whicher's reputation never recovered. Five years later Constance confessed that, alone and unaided, she had murdered her half-brother.

I think it would be going too far to see the Road Hill House case itself as directly influencing the development of detective fiction, but the national reaction to the crime at the time certainly confirmed the Victorian interest in sensational murders and in the process of detection. Largely because Constance Kent's confession, although accepted by the court, could not possibly have been completely true, interest in the case has never ceased and there have been a number of well-documented accounts.

The crime also inspired later novelists, including Dickens, and as late as 1983 Francis King transferred the story to India during the period of the British Raj in his novel *Act of Darkness*. The most recent account is by Kate Summerscale in *The Suspicions of Mr. Whicher*, which concentrates on the investigation of the murder and provides fascinating details of the extraordinary public response to the crime and the subsequent lives of those concerned. Kate Summerscale also provides a solution to the mystery which I find convincing.

It seems now that all the participants in the tragedy and the general public were enacting in advance and in real life the storyline of detective novels which were to become common in the interwar years: the mysterious murder, the closed circle of suspects, the isolated rural community, the respectable and prosperous setting and the brilliant detective called in from outside to solve the crime when the local police are baffled. An age so fascinated by violence, both in real life and in literature, so ready to involve itself with relish in the process of detection, was certainly ready for the advent of the man who is commonly regarded as the first great British fictional detective and who was to appear in 1887 with the publication of Arthur Conan Doyle's *A Study in Scarlet.*

The Tenant of 221B Baker Street and the Parish Priest from Cobhole in Essex

You mentioned your name, as if I should recognize it, but I assure you that, beyond the obvious facts that you are a bachelor, a solicitor, a Freemason, and an asthmatic, I know nothing whatever about you.

Arthur Conan Doyle, "The Adventure of the Norwood Builder"

I T I S a safe assumption that enthusiasts for detective fiction, whatever their country or nationality, if asked to name the three most famous fictional detectives, will begin with Sherlock Holmes. In the long list of amateur sleuths down the last nine decades, he remains unique, the unchallenged Great Detective, whose brilliant deductive intelligence could outwit any adversary, however cunning, and solve any

"I must say, Mr. Baskerville, we had expected something larger."

puzzle, however bizarre. In the decades following his creator's death in 1930, he has become an icon.

When Arthur Conan Doyle published *A Study in Scarlet* he was a newly married general practitioner living in Southsea with ambitions to become a writer, but so far with better success in medicine than in fiction, despite being both prolific and hard-working. Then, in 1886, came the idea which was to bear fruit beyond his imagination. He decided to try his luck with a detective story, but one markedly different from the tales then being published, which he thought unimaginative, unfair in their denouement, and whose detectives were mere stereotypes who depended for success more on luck and the stupidity of the criminal than their own cleverness. His detective would employ scientific methods and logical deduction. *A Study in Scarlet* was first published in 1887 as one contribution in *Beeton's Christmas Annual*, priced at one shilling. The annual was hugely popular and quickly sold out, but the story was not widely reviewed, gaining only a few mentions in the national press. A year later *A Study in Scarlet* was published as a separate volume, and reprinted in 1889. Conan Doyle, however, gained very little from this attempt at detective fiction, having relinquished all rights in his story for twenty-five pounds. But it is here in his first detective story, seen through the eyes of his friend and flatmate Dr. Watson, that the great detective is brought clearly before us in an image which, with the addition of his deerstalker hat and pipe, has remained fixed in the public imagination.

In height he was rather over six feet, and so excessively lean that he seemed to be considerably taller. His eyes were sharp and piercing, save during those intervals of torpor to which I have alluded; and his thin hawk-like nose gave his whole expression an air of alertness and decision. His chin, too, had the prominence and squareness which mark the man of determination. His hands were invariably blotted with ink and stained with chemicals, yet he was possessed of extraordinary delicacy of touch, as I frequently had occasion to observe when I watched him manipulating his fragile philosophical instruments.

And it is in *A Study in Scarlet* that Holmes himself gives proof of his deductive powers.

"There has been murder done, and the murderer was a man. He was more than six feet high, was in the prime of life, had small feet for his height, wore coarse, square-toed boots and smoked a Trichinopoly cigar. He came here with his victim in a four-wheeled cab, which was drawn by a horse with three old shoes and one new one on his off foreleg. In all probability the murderer had a florid face, and the fingernails of his right hand were remarkably long. These are only a few indications but they may assist you."

Lestrade and Gregson glanced at each other with an incredulous smile.

"If this man was murdered, how was it done?" asked the former.

"Poison," said Sherlock Holmes curtly, and strode off.

Despite the amount of detailed information about Holmes and his habits provided by Watson in the short stories, the core of the man remains elusive. He is obviously clever with a practical, rational, non-threatening intelligence, patriotic, compassionate, resourceful and brave—qualities which mirror those of his creator. This is not surprising, since writers who create a serial character inevitably endow him or her with their own interests and preoccupations. Conan Doyle admitted that "a man cannot spin a character out of his own inner consciousness and make it really life-like unless he has some possibilities of that character within him." Even so, I would have expected him to have been more attached to the valiant Dr. Watson, wounded hero of the second Afghan war, than to this unsentimental, neurotic and cocaine-injecting genius of deduction. Holmes is a violinist, so he is not without a cultural interest, but we are probably unwise to accept Watson's partial view of the measure of his talent. Although the call to a new case provokes in Holmes a surge of enthusiasm and physical and mental energy, he has a doubting and pessimistic streak, and more than a touch of modern cynicism. "What you do in this world is a matter of no consequence. The question is, what you can make people believe you have done" (*A Study in Scarlet*). "We reach. We grasp. And what is left in our hands at the end? A shadow. Or worse than a shadow—misery" ("The Adventure of the Retired Colourman"). In this too Holmes could be reflecting a dichotomy in his own character, and indeed one aspect of Victorian sensibility. He is of his age but, curiously, also of ours, and this too may be part of the secret of his lasting appeal.

The inspiration for Sherlock Holmes was Dr. Joseph Bell, a consultant surgeon at the Edinburgh Royal Infirmary whose reputation as a brilliant diagnostician was based on his ability to observe closely and interpret the apparently insignificant facts presented by the appearance and habits of his patients. Conan Doyle also acknowledged the influence of Edgar Allan Poe, who was born in 1809 and died in 1849, and whose detective, Chevalier C. Auguste Dupin, was the first fictional investigator to rely primarily on deduction from observable facts. Many critics would argue that the main credit for inventing the detective story and influencing its development should be shared by Conan Doyle and Poe. Poe is chiefly remembered for his tales of the macabre, but in four short stories alone he introduced what were to become the stock plot devices of early detective stories. "The Murders in the Rue Morgue" (1841) is a locked-room mystery. In "The Mystery of Marie Rogêt" (1842) the detective solves the crime from newspaper cuttings and press reports, making this the first example of armchair detection. In "The Purloined Letter" (1844) we have an example of the perpetrator being the most unlikely suspect, a ploy which was to become common with Agatha Christie and in danger of becoming a cliché, so that readers whose main interest in the story was to correctly identify the murderer had only to fix on the least likely suspect to be sure of success. "The Gold-Bug" makes use of cryptography in solving the crime; so too did Dorothy L. Sayers, both in *Have His Carcase* and in *The Nine Tailors*. Poe did not describe himself as a detective writer, but both he and his hero, C. Auguste Dupin, have their rightful importance in the history of the genre, although Dupin cannot challenge the dominance of Sherlock Holmes and has little in common with Holmes except for their deductive skills. Sherlock Holmes remains unique. We may not feel personally drawn to his eccentricities, but generations have entered into his world and have shared the excitement, entertainment and pure reading pleasure of his adventures. Conan Doyle was a superb storyteller, the Sherlock Holmes canon is still in print and the stories are being read by new generations nearly eighty years after Conan Doyle's death.

No writer who achieves spectacular success does so without a modicum of good luck. For Conan Doyle this occurred when he was invited to contribute a series of self-contained short stories for *Strand Magazine*, founded by George Newnes in 1891. *The Strand* broke new ground, attracting readers with such innovations as interviews with celebrities, general articles, photographs and free gifts, foreshadowing the popular magazines which were to prosper in the next century. With a readership of over 300,000 it provided Conan Doyle with a double bonus: not only could he be assured of a huge and growing public, but he was now able to concentrate on short stories, the form which suited him best. Today such good fortune could only be equated to a long-running major television series. This too, posthumously, he gained. To add to his wide exposure during his author's lifetime, the exploits of Sherlock Holmes have been a gift to radio, television and film, and millions of viewers have thrilled to *The Hound of the Baskervilles* who have never read the novel. His success was also helped by the talent of his illustrator, Sidney Paget, who created Holmes's handsome but sternly authoritative features and clothed him in the deerstalker hat and caped coat, a picture which has formed the mental image of the great detective for generations.

Conan Doyle also had the good fortune to

publish when his own character, his literary talent and his hero met the needs and expectations of his age. The Sherlock Holmes saga provided for an increasingly literate society and the emergence of an upper working and middle class with leisure to read who welcomed stories which were original, accessible, exciting and with that occasional frisson of horror to which the Victorians were never averse. Conan Doyle was himself a representative of his sex and class. He was a man his fellow countrymen could understand: a stalwart imperialist, patriotic, courageous, resourceful and with the self-confidence to congratulate himself on having "the strongest influence over young men, especially young athletic sporting men, than anyone in England, bar Kipling." But his most attractive characteristic was undoubtedly his passion for justice, and he was indefatigable in spending time, money and energy in righting injustices wherever they came to light. He imbued Sherlock Holmes with the same passion, the same courage.

But despite the excellent qualities which Holmes shared with his creator, Watson's description of him gives a picture of a somewhat unlikely hero. In enumerating the limits of his flatmate's interests, Watson states that his knowledge of literature was nil, although he appeared to know every detail of every horror perpetrated in the century and his reading of sensational literature was immense. In the Victorian controversy between the somewhat despised "sensational business" and the reputable straight novel, there is no doubt where Holmes's interests lay. It was his declared policy not to acquire any knowledge which was not useful to him or would not bear upon his job. He was an expert boxer and swordsman and had a good practical knowledge of the law and of poisons, including belladonna and opium. Although exhaustively energetic when engaged on a case, he spent days lying on a sofa without uttering a word, regularly injected himself with cocaine, and with his erratic lifestyle and habit of firing off his revolver in the sitting-room to pattern the wall with bullet holes must have been an uncomfortable and sometimes dangerous companion for his friend and flatmate Dr. Watson. Mrs. Hudson was certainly a most accommodating landlady.

A moment of Holmes-like deduction suggests that, if there is a 221B, there must be a 221A, and possibly a 221C. What did the tenants above and below think of having their peace disturbed by Sherlock Holmes's patriotic shooting practice or the mysterious and odd people who regularly came to his door? And why did such a brilliant and successful investigator, called on by the rich and famous, able to afford a special train to take Dr. Watson and himself to the scene of crime, need to share lodgings in what seems to be essentially a rooming house? We are told by Dr. Watson in *A Study in Scarlet* that the accommodation at 221B Baker Street "consisted of a couple of comfortable bedrooms and a single large airy sitting-room, cheerfully furnished and illuminated by two broad windows." So desirable in every way were the apartments, and so moderate the terms when divided between the two men, "that the bargain was concluded upon the spot." We also learn that the sitting-room was Sherlock Holmes's office and the place where he received his visitors, which meant that Watson had to be banished to his bedroom when anyone arrived on business, which was not infrequently. It hardly seems a satisfactory arrangement and I am not surprised that eventually, despite the moderate cost, Watson moved out. And was this really a feasible arrangement for Sherlock Holmes, who couldn't have been a poor man? One of his clients was the King of Sardinia, and noblemen as well as the humble workers of the world came to that sitting-room for help. In "The Adventure of the Priory School," Holmes finds Lord Saltire, the son of the Duke of Holdernesse, who was missing from his preparatory school, and receives as his fee a cheque for ten thousand pounds—in those days a small fortune. He folds up the cheque and places it carefully in his notebook with the comment, "I am a poor man." But poor he certainly was not. Was he perhaps a secret philanthropist who used his income from prosperous clients to subsidise the poor? He couldn't have spent money on a main and more luxurious home, since his frequent absences to return to it would undoubtedly have been commented upon by Dr. Watson. And what happened to Dr. Watson's dog? Before moving into 221B he confesses that he keeps a bull pup, but we never hear again about this animal. Did Mrs. Hudson put down her foot, or was the unfortunate puppy a victim of Sherlock Holmes's revolver practice? But for me the greater mystery has to be the missing money. I have no doubt, however, that all will later be explained to me by members of the worldwide Sherlock Holmes societies, by whom no detail of Holmes's life or cases, and no discrepancies in the plots, have been left unexamined.

In addition to his four full-length novels—*A*

Study in Scarlet, The Sign of Four, The Hound of the Baskervilles and *The Valley of Fear*—Conan Doyle published five collections of short stories featuring his hero. With such a large output, the quality is inevitably sometimes uneven. A number of the stories are frankly incredible, an example being one of the most popular and best known, "The Speckled Band." It is also among the most terrifying. Here we encounter the most evil of Holmes's adversaries, Dr. Rylott, who from his first entrance in 221B Baker Street reveals his strength and brutality. As a doctor, he surely had the means to dispose of his step-daughter with expedience and safety, but the method he employed somehow seems a wanton wish on his part to make the investigation as complicated as possible for Holmes, rather than a rational plan to commit a successful murder. There are other inconsistencies in a number of the stories, but I have some sympathy with the judgement of the late novelist and critic Julian Symons that we should not fall into the error of preferring technical perfection to brilliant storytelling, and that if one were choosing the best twenty short detective stories ever written, at least half a dozen would feature Sherlock Holmes.

Holmes's lasting attraction also derives from

the setting and atmosphere of the stories. We enter into that Victorian world of fog and gaslight, the jingle of horses' reins, the grind of wheels on cobblestones and the shadow of a veiled woman climbing the stairs to that claustrophobic sanctum at 221B Baker Street. Such is the power of the writing that it is we, the readers, who conjure up this enveloping miasma of mystery and terror. *The Sign of Four* mentions a dense, drizzly fog, but the weather is rarely described except briefly in phrases like "a bleak windy day towards the end of March," or "a close rainy day in October." We provide what our imaginations need, including the detail of the small sitting-room, the untidiness, the initials VR in bullet marks in the wall and the smell of Holmes's pipe. We may not always believe in the details of the plot, but we always believe in the man himself and the world he inhabits.

And the magic has remained. We readers, in our fidelity to Holmes, have a greater respect for him than had his creator. Conan Doyle was a man of high literary ambition and, although he was too good a craftsman not to take care over the Holmes stories, he didn't take them seriously and had every intention of killing off his hero when the first series ended, so that he could devote himself to what he saw as more prestigious literature. It was at the end of the second series of stories that he decided to kill both Holmes and his adversary, Moriarty, by plunging them over the Reichenbach Falls. But Holmes was not so easy to kill and by public demand was reinstated, although some readers may feel that the great detective was never quite the same man after the Reichenbach experience. Conan Doyle could not resist the public clamour for Holmes to be saved, nor say no to the enormous fees he was earning. But he still deplored the egregious success of his detective and wrote to his friend, "I have had such an overdose of him that I feel towards him as I do towards *pâté-de-foie-gras*, of which I once ate too much, so that the name of it gives me a sickly feeling to this day." But the readers did, and indeed still do, feast on the Holmes short stories not with nausea but with renewed appetite.

Another Victorian whose influence and reputation have been almost as great, in my view deservedly, was as prolific as Conan Doyle but very different both as a man and as a writer. Gilbert Keith Chesterton, who was born on Campden Hill in London in 1874 and died in 1936, can be described in terms which are hardly ever used of a writer today: he was a man of letters. All his life he earned his living by his pen and he was as versatile as he was prolific, gaining a reputation as a novelist, essayist, critic, journalist and poet. Much of this output, particularly on social, political and religious subjects, has proved ephemeral, but a few of his poems, including "The Donkey" and "The Rolling English Road," continue to appear in anthologies of popular verse. But he is chiefly remembered as one of the most brilliant writers of the short detective story and for his serial detective, the Roman Catholic priest Father Brown. *The Innocence of Father Brown* was published in 1911 and was followed by four further volumes; the last, *The Scandal of Father Brown*, appeared in 1935. G. K. Chesterton converted to Roman Catholicism in 1922, and his faith became central to his life and work. His fictional priest was based on his friend Father John O'Connor, to whom *The Secret of Father Brown*, published in 1927, was dedicated.

We first meet Father Brown in the story "The Blue Cross," and see him through the eyes of Valentin, described as the head of the Paris police. Valentin found himself sharing a railway carriage with a very short Roman Catholic priest going up from a small Essex village, who seemed to Valentin to be "the essence of those Eastern

43

flats with a face as round and dull as a Norfolk dumpling and eyes as empty as the North Sea." He had several brown-paper parcels which he was quite incapable of managing, a large shabby umbrella which constantly fell on the floor, and did not seem to know which was the right part of his return ticket. Valentin was not the only person to be taken in by this seeming innocence and simplicity.

Father Brown could not be more different from the Golden Age heroes of detective fiction. He worked alone with no routine police support, as had Lord Peter Wimsey with Inspector Parker, no Watson to provide an admiring audience and to ask questions on behalf of the less perspicacious readers, and without even Holmes's limited scientific knowledge. He solved crimes by a mixture of common sense, observation and his knowledge of the human heart. As he says to Flambeau, the master thief whom he outwits in "The Blue Cross" and whom he restores to honesty, "Has it never struck you that a man who does next to nothing but hear men's real sins is not likely to be wholly unaware of human evil?" There were, of course, other advantages of being a priest: he was never required to explain precisely why he was present because it was assumed that he was occupied with his priestly function, and he was a man in whom many might naturally confide.

Although we are told that Father Brown was parish priest in Cobhole in Essex before moving to London, we meet him in other and very different places, in England and overseas, and in a variety of settings and company across the whole social and economic spectrum. Nothing and no one is alien to him. We rarely encounter him in the daily routine of his pastoral duties at Cobhole, never learn where exactly he lives, who housekeeps for him, what kind of church he has or his relationship with his bishop. We are not told his age, whether his parents are still living or even his Christian name. In each of the stories he makes his quiet appearance unannounced, as much at home with the poor and humble as he is with the rich and famous, and applying to all situations his own immutable spirituality. But he is always a rationalist with a dislike of superstition, which he sees as inimical to his faith. Like the other characters in the stories—and like us, the readers—he sees the physical facts of the case, but only he, by a process of deduction, interprets them correctly. In this he resembles, in his methods, Sherlock Holmes and Hercule Poirot. We see what is apparently obvious, however bizarre; he sees what is true. Chesterton loved paradox and, because we encounter Father Brown often in incongruous company and he comes unencumbered by his past, the little priest is himself a paradox, at once endearingly human, but also a mysterious and iconic harbinger of death.

G. K. Chesterton's output was prodigious, and it would be unreasonable to expect all the short stories to be equally successful, but the quality of the writing never disappoints. Chesterton never wrote an inelegant or clumsy sentence. The Father Brown stories are written in a style richly complex, imaginative, vigorous, poetic and spiced with paradoxes. He had been trained as an artist and he saw life with an artist's eye. He wanted his readers to share that poetic vision, to see the romance and numinousness in commonplace things. He brought two things in particular to detective fiction. He was among the first writers to realise that it could be a vehicle for exploring and exposing the condition of society, and for saying something true about human nature. Before he even planned the Father Brown stories, Chesterton wrote that "the only thrill, even of a common thriller, is concerned somehow with the conscience and the will." Those words have been part of my credo as a writer. They may not be framed and on my desk but they are never out of my mind.

In *Bloody Murder*, published in 1972, revised in 1985 and again in 1992, a book which has become essential reading for many aficionados of crime fiction, Julian Symons suggests that because of their richness, no more than a few Father Brown short stories should be read at a time. Certainly to settle down for an evening with Father Brown would be like facing a meal composed entirely of very rich *hors d'œuvres*, but I have never suffered from literary indigestion when reading the stories, partly because of Chesterton's imaginative power and his all-embracing humanity. At the end of the short story "The Invisible Man" we are told that Flambeau and the other participants in the mystery went back to their ordinary lives. "But Father Brown walked those snow-covered hills under the stars for many hours with a murderer, and what they said to each other will never be known." We can be sure that, whatever was spoken, it had little or nothing to do with the criminal justice system.

"Your red herring. My Lord."

3

The Golden Age

When one looks at the Golden Age in retrospect
the developing rebellion against its ideas and stan-
dards is clearly visible, but this is the wisdom of
hindsight, for during the thirties the classical detective story burgeoned with new and considerable talents almost every year.

Julian Symons, Bloody Murder

A VICTORIAN CRITIC of the Sherlock
Holmes stories, writing in *Blackwood's
Magazine* in the late 1800s, while not
altogether dismissive of the saga, concluded with
the words: "Considering the difficulty of hitting
on any fancies that are decently fresh, surely this
sensational business must shortly come to a
close." No prophecy could have been more mis-
judged. Not only did the sensational business
continue, but the new century saw an outburst
of creative energy directed towards detective fiction, the emergence of new talented writers and a

public which greeted their efforts with an avid enthusiasm which contemporary cartoons suggest amounted to a craze. Although short stories continued to be written, gradually they gave way to the detective novel. One reason for this change was probably because the writers and their increasingly enthusiastic readers preferred a longer narrative, which gave opportunities for even more complicated plotting and more fully developed characters. In the words of G. K. Chesterton, "The long story is more successful, perhaps, in one not unimportant point: that it is possible to realise that a man is alive before he is dead." Novelists, too, if visited by a powerful idea for an original method of murder, detective or plotline, were unwilling—and indeed still are— to dissipate it on a short story when it could both inspire and form the main interest of a successful novel.

The well-known description "Golden Age" is commonly taken to cover the two decades between the First and Second World Wars, but this limitation is unduly restrictive. One of the most famous detective stories regarded as falling within the Golden Age is *Trent's Last Case* by E. C. Bentley, published in 1913. The name of this novel is familiar to many readers who have never read it, and its importance is partly due to the respect with which it was regarded by practitioners of the time and its influence on the genre. Dorothy L. Sayers wrote that it "holds a very special place in the history of detective fiction, a tale of unusual brilliance and charm, startlingly original." Agatha Christie saw it as "one of the three best detective stories ever written." Edgar Wallace described it as "a masterpiece of detective fiction," and G. K. Chesterton saw it as "the finest detective story of modern times." Today some of the tributes of his contemporaries seem excessive but the novel remains highly readable, if hardly as compelling as it was when first published, and its influence on the Golden Age is unquestionable. E. C. Bentley, who wrote the book between 1910 and 1912, was a lifelong friend and fellow journalist of G. K. Chesterton and probably wrote the novel with Chesterton's encouragement. But what Bentley produced was hardly what his friend would have expected. Seeing himself as a modernist, Bentley disliked the conventional straitjacket of the orthodox detective story and had little respect for Sherlock Holmes. He planned a small act of sabotage, a detective story which was to satirize rather than celebrate the genre. It is ironic that although his hero, Trent, doesn't solve the murder—nor of course did Sergeant Cuff in *The Moonstone*—Bentley is seen as an innovator, not a destroyer of the detective story.

The victim in *Trent's Last Case* is an American multimillionaire, an exploiter of the poor and a ruthless financial buccaneer who is found dead in the grounds of his country house with a bullet through the eye. The detective is an amateur sleuth and a painter, Philip Trent, and only at the end of the book do we know why this is his last case. The clues are fairly presented and there is at the end not one surprising disclosure, but two. The novel is unusual in that Trent falls in love with the victim's widow, Mabel Manderson, and unlike many of the novelists of the Golden Age, Bentley was as concerned with the portrayal of character, particularly that of Manderson, as he was with providing a coherent and exciting puzzle. The dominance of the love interest was also unusual. Subsequent writers tended to agree with Dorothy L. Sayers that their detectives should concentrate their energy on clues and not on chasing attractive young women. The book is also original in that Trent's solution to the mystery, although based on the clues available, proves erroneous. The fact that the detective hero doesn't solve the crime, though offending against what many see as the prime unwritten rule of detective fiction, certainly makes *Trent's Last Case* innovative.

Writing about the novel in *Bloody Murder*, Julian Symons struggles to understand the regard in which many hold the novel, largely because of the dichotomy between the opening paragraphs, which deal with an ironic savagery with Manderson's murder, and the change of mood in the second part. There is also an uncertainty in Bentley's characterisation of Trent, who at times is almost a figure of fun, and yet whose love affair is treated with great seriousness and so, far from being a diversion to the detective element, is cleverly integrated with the plot. Nevertheless, instead of being later regarded as an iconoclastic or ironic novel, *Trent's Last Case* was seen as perhaps the most significant and successful immediate precursor of the Golden Age.

The writers of the Golden Age attracted to this fascinating form were as varied as their talents. It must at times have seemed as if everyone who could put together a coherent narrative was compelled to have a go at this challenging and lucrative craft. Many writers who made a reputation for detective fiction already had successful careers in other fields. Nicholas Blake, whose detective is Nigel Strangeways, was the poet Cecil Day-Lewis (1904–1972). Edmund Crispin was the pseudonym of Robert Bruce Montgomery (1921–1978), a musician, composer and critic. Cyril Hare was Judge Alfred Alexander Gordon Clark (1900–1958). Monsignor Ronald Knox (1888–1957) wrote under his own name, as did G. D. H. Cole (1889–1959) and his wife, Margaret (1893–1980), who were both economists. These novelists, already successful in other fields, produced books which have a liveliness, humour and distinction of style which places them well above what Julian Symons categorises as "the humdrums." They seem, indeed, to have been written as much for the amusement of the author as for the entertainment of his readers. Michael Innes, the pseudonym of John Innes Mackintosh Stewart (1906–1994), was an Oxford don and Professor of English at the University of Adelaide for ten years. His detective, Sir John Appleby of Scotland Yard, is one of the earliest, possibly the first, of that group of academic sleuths who are sometimes referred to as "dons' delights." Appleby is, however, very far from an amateur, having begun his career in the police and progressed naturally through the ranks from inspector to the highest rank, Commissioner of the Metropolitan Police, a promotion which I find somewhat hard to believe. Innes produced in Appleby probably the most erudite of all fictional detectives in books which are witty, literate, larded with quotations chosen to be unfamiliar to all but learned academics and with plots which are sometimes more bizarre than credible. One of the most interesting aspects of Appleby is the way in which he ages and matures so that readers who fall under his spell can have the satisfaction of vicariously living his life. From his first case, the murder of Dr. Umbleby in 1936, to that of Lord Osprey in 1986, no other detective writer has produced for his hero such a well-documented life, including Appleby's retirement. This is very rare. Although I admire Ian Rankin's temerity in allowing Detective Inspector John Rebus to retire, most of us with a serial hero are content to take refuge in the fashionable illusion that our detectives are immutably fixed in the first age we assigned to them; although in a moment of disillusion they may talk of retiring, they seldom actually do so.

Other prominent academics joined in the game, perhaps intrigued by the challenge set by the rules which were laid down by Ronald Knox in the preface to *Best Detective Stories 1928–29*, which he edited. The criminal must be mentioned in the early part of the narrative but must not be anyone whose thoughts the reader has been allowed to follow. All supernatural agencies are ruled out. There must not be more than one secret room or passage. No hitherto undiscovered poisons should be used or, indeed, any appliance which needs a long scientific explanation. No Chinamen must figure in the story. No accident must help the detective, nor is he allowed an unaccountable intuition. The detective himself must not commit the crime or alight on any clues which are not instantly produced for the reader. The stupid friend of the detective, the Watson, should be slightly, but no more than slightly, less intelligent than the average reader, and his thoughts should not be concealed. And, finally, twin brothers and doubles generally must not appear unless the reader has been duly prepared for them.

These rules, if accepted as mandatory, would have reduced the detective story to a quasi-intellectual puzzle in which the reader would be exercising his intelligence, not only against the fictional murderer, but against the writer, whose quirks and cunning ploys aficionados set out to recognise and confute. Rules and restrictions do not produce original, or good, literature, and the rules were not strictly adhered to. The Watson became superfluous relatively soon and, having a tendency, indeed an obligation, to be boring, was rarely missed. But writers obviously felt the need to have a character to whom the detective could communicate, however slightly, the progress of his investigation, as much for the reader's benefit as for his own, and commonly a servant provided this convenient expedient. Dorothy L. Sayers's Lord Peter Wimsey had Bunter and could of course discuss the progress of the case with his brother-in-law, Chief Inspector Parker. Margery Allingham's Albert Campion had his cockney manservant, Magersfontein Lugg, but Lugg seems designed more as comic relief than a sounding board for his master's theories, and Campion, who frequently worked with the police, could rely more rationally on Inspector Stanislaus Oates and Charlie Luke. After the departure of Captain Hastings, Agatha Christie's Poirot made something of a confidant of Chief Inspector Japp, but otherwise both he and Miss Marple preferred to work in isolation, their reticence broken only by their occasional enigmatic hints and comments.

One rule was brilliantly broken by Agatha

Christie, arch-breaker of rules, in her long-running play *The Mousetrap*. She perpetrated an even more audacious deception on the reader in *The Murder of Roger Ackroyd*, where the narrator proves to be the murderer, an ingenious if defensible defiance of all the rules, and although she provided perfectly fair clues, some readers have never forgiven her. The prohibition against Chinamen is difficult to understand. Or was it perhaps the general view that Chinamen, if inclined to murder, would be so clever and cunning in their villainy that the famous detective would be unfairly hampered in his investigation? It is possible that Monsignor Knox was obliquely referring to Dr. Fu Manchu, that oriental genius of crime created by Sax Rohmer, who for nearly fifty years between 1912 and 1959 pursued his evil purposes while no doubt contributing to racial prejudice and fear of the menacing Yellow Peril.

The first rule is interesting. Certainly a proper regard to structure and balance would suggest that the murderer should make an appearance comparatively early in the story, but a demand that this should be no later than two-thirds of the way through the narrative seems unduly restrictive. Some novelists like to begin either with a murder or with the discovery of the body, an exciting and shocking beginning that not only sets the mood of the novel but involves the reader immediately in drama and action. Although I have used this method with some of my novels, I have more commonly chosen to defer the crime and begin by establishing the setting and by introducing my readers to the victim, the murderer, the suspects, and the life of the community in which the murder will take place. This has the advantage that the setting can be described with more leisure than is practicable once the action is under way, and that many of the facts about the suspects and their possible motives are known and do not have to be revealed at length during the course of the investigation. Deferring the actual murder, apart from the build-up of tension, also ensures that the reader is in possession of more information than is the detective when he arrives at the scene. It is an inviolable rule that the detective should never know more than the reader, but there is no injunction against the reader knowing more than the detective—including, of course, when a particular suspect is lying.

With his rule that the reader should not be allowed to follow the murderer's thoughts, Monsignor Knox raises one of the main problems in writing mystery fiction. In an introduction to an anthology of short stories published in 1928, Dorothy L. Sayers confronted this difficulty, which still challenges detective novelists today. Miss Sayers did nothing in her life by halves. Having decided to earn some much-needed money by writing detective fiction, she applied her mind to the history, technique and possibilities of the genre. Being highly intelligent, opinionated and combative, she had no hesitation in giving other people the advantage of her views. Not surprisingly, it is Sayers to whom we frequently look for an expert view on the problems and challenges of writing detective fiction in the Golden Age. She wrote:

> It does not—and by hypothesis never can—attain the loftiest level of literary achievement. Though it deals with the most desperate effects of rage, jealousy and revenge, it rarely touches the heights and depths of human passion. It presents us only with a *fait accompli* and looks upon death and mutilation with a dispassionate eye. It does not show us the inner workings of the murderer's mind; it must not, for the identity of the murderer is hidden until the end of the book.

If the detective story is to be more than an ingenious puzzle, the murderer must be more than a conventional cardboard stereotype to be knocked down in the last chapter, and the writer who can solve the problem of enabling the reader at some point to share the murderer's compulsions and inner life, so that he becomes more than a necessary character to serve the plot, will have a chance of writing a novel which is more than a lifeless if entertaining conundrum.

The majority of the Golden Age novels are at present out of print, but the names of the most popular still resonate; their crumbling paperbacks can still be seen on the racks of secondhand bookstores or in private libraries where their owners are reluctant finally to dispose of old friends who have given so much half-remembered pleasure. Those writers who are still read have provided something more than an exciting and original plot: distinction in the writing, a vivid sense of place, a memorable and compelling hero and—most important of all—the ability to draw the reader into their highly individual world.

The omni-talented amateur with apparently nothing to do with his time but solve murders which interest him has had his day, partly because his rich and privileged lifestyle became less admirable, and his deferential acceptance by the police less credible, in an age when men were expected to work. Increasingly the private eye had a profession, or occasionally some connection with the police. Doctors were popular and were usually provided with some idiosyncratic hobby or habit, an interest for which they had plenty of time since we rarely saw them with a patient. Among the most popular was H. C. Bailey's detective Reggie Fortune, MA, MB, BSc, FRCS, who first appeared in 1920 in *Call Mr. Fortune*. Reggie is a weighty character in both senses of the word, a gourmet, the husband of an exceptionally beautiful wife and a doughty defender of the weak and vulnerable, particularly children. Occasionally his concern as a social reformer in these fields tended to override the detective element. His whimsicality and distinctly odd elliptical style of speaking could be irritating, but the fact that he featured in ninety-five detective stories, the last published in 1946, is a measure of his readers' loyalty.

Perhaps the most eccentric doctor detective of the interwar years is Dame Beatrice Adela Lestrange Bradley, Gladys Mitchell's psychiatrist who first appeared in 1929 in *Speedy Death*.

Thereafter Miss Mitchell published a book a year, sometimes two, until 1984. Dame Beatrice was a true original: elderly, bizarre in dress and appearance, with the eyes of a crocodile. Professionally she was highly regarded, despite the fact that her methods seemed more intuitive than scientific, and although we are told she was consultant to the Home Office it is not clear whether this entailed treating any home secretary whose peculiarities were causing concern, or involving herself with convicted criminals, which seems equally unlikely. In either case she had plenty of time to be driven round the country in style by George, her chauffeur, and to involve herself in such interests as Roman ruins, the occult, ancient Greek mysticism and the Loch Ness Monster. There are frequent allusions to her mysterious past—a distant ancestor was apparently a witch—and she was much given to conclusions which seem to owe more to her esoteric knowledge than to logical deduction. Like Reggie Fortune, she had a maverick attitude toward authority. I remember enjoying the best of the novels because of Miss Mitchell's style, although I frequently found the stories confusing and occasionally yearned for the rationality which surely lies at the heart of detective fiction.

Three writers whose books have deservedly lasted beyond the Golden Age and can still be found in print are Edmund Crispin, Cyril Hare and Josephine Tey. Each had a profession apart from writing, and each produced one book which has generally proved the favourite among their work. Edmund Crispin, following his time at St. John's College, Oxford, where he was part of the generation which included Kingsley Amis, spent two years as an organ scholar and choirmaster. Like many other detective writers, he made excellent use of his personal experience, both of Oxford and of his career as a musician. His hero is Gervase Fen, Professor of English Language and Literature at St. Christopher's College, who made his appearance in 1944 with *The Case of the Gilded Fly.* Gervase Fen is a true original, a ruddy-faced man with unruly hair, much given to witticisms and, appropriately enough, quotations from the classics, who romps through his cases with infectious *joie de vivre* in books which are genuinely very funny. We meet his wife, Dolly, a placid comfortable lady who sits peacefully knitting, apparently undisturbed by her husband's propensity for investigating murder, and who takes no part in his adventures, contenting herself by reminding him not to wake the children when he returns home. We learn nothing of the sex of these children and are only surprised that Professor Fen has found the time and energy to father them. He seems to be rarely inconvenienced by academic duties and in one book, *Buried for Pleasure* (1948), he becomes a parliamentary candidate, narrowly escaping what for him would have been the inconvenience of being elected. Crispin's most ingenious book is generally regarded as *The Moving Toyshop* (1946), which begins when the young poet Richard Cadogan, arriving late at night in Oxford, casually opens an unlocked door and finds himself in a toyshop with the dead body of a woman on the floor. Reasonably, he summons the police, but they arrive to find no toyshop and no corpse. Fen joins forces with Cadogan and they clatter through Oxford in Fen's old car, "Lily Christine," causing maximum damage and disturbance to the populace in their determination to solve the mystery.

Crispin's books are always elegantly written with a cast of engaging, witty characters. Most readers at some point in the story will laugh aloud. Crispin is a farceur, and the ability successfully to combine this less-than-subtle humour with murder is very rare in detective fiction. One modern writer who comes to mind is Simon

Brett, whose hero—if the word can be regarded as appropriate—Charles Paris is an unsuccessful and hard-drinking actor separated from his wife. Like Edmund Crispin, Simon Brett makes use of his own experience—in his case as a playwright for radio and television—and, like Crispin, he can combine humour with a credible mystery solved by an original and believable private eye.

Cyril Hare was a barrister who became a county court judge; he took his writing name from his London home, Cyril Mansions in Battersea, and his chambers in Hare Court. Like Edmund Crispin, he made effective use of his professional experience and expertise, creating in his hero, Francis Pettigrew, a humane, intelligent but not particularly successful barrister who, unlike Professor Fen, is a reluctant rather than avid amateur detective. Like Crispin he has a felicitous style, and his humour, although less laughter-provoking, has wit and subtlety. His best-known book—and, I would argue, by far the most successful—is *Tragedy at Law*, published in 1942. This novel, which is happily in print, is also something of a period piece, since we the readers move with the Honourable Sir William Hereward Barber, a judge of the High Court of Justice, as he travels round the towns of the South West

Circuit. This perambulation in great state of an assize judge has now been abolished with the creation of the Crown Court; as the book is set in the early days of the Second World War, we have the interest both of fairly recent history and of a now dead tradition. The plot is well worked out, credible and, as with the majority of his books, rests on the provisions of the law. Like Crispin's, the writing is lively, the dialogue convincing, the characters interesting and the plot involving. The book opens with a loud complaint by the judge that, because of the economies of war, his appearance is not being celebrated as it should be with a flourish of trumpets. The man, the time and the place are immediately set in an opening paragraph which is as arresting as if the trumpets had indeed sounded.

Josephine Tey, the pseudonym of the Scottish writer Elizabeth Mackintosh (1896–1952), was better known in her lifetime for her play *Richard of Bordeaux* than she was for her detective fiction. Her detective is Inspector Alan Grant, who is very much in the gentlemanly mould, notable for his intuition, intelligence and Scottish tenacity. He first appeared in *The Man in the Queue* (1929) and was still on the job when, in 1952, Tey published her eighth and last crime novel, *The*

Singing Sands. But with the two novels which many readers regard as among her best, *Brat Farrar* (1949) and *The Franchise Affair* (1948), she moved further from the conventional plot of the detective story and with such success that she might not now be regarded as a detective novelist had she not created Inspector Grant. Novelists who prefer not to be so designated should beware of introducing a serial detective.

Brat Farrar is a mystery of identity set on the estate and the riding stables of Latchetts on the south coast. If Patrick Ashby, heir to the property, has really committed suicide, who is the mysterious young man calling himself Brat Farrar who returns to claim the family inheritance, who not only looks like Patrick but is familiar with details of the family history? We, the readers, know that he is an impostor, although we quickly come to sympathise with him. This, then, is a mystery of identification, common in English fiction, and the fact that *Brat Farrar* is also a murder mystery only becomes apparent late in the novel. In what is probably Tey's best-known book, *The Franchise Affair*, two eccentric newcomers to the village, an elderly widow and her spinster daughter, are accused by a young woman of imprisoning her in their isolated house, The Franchise, and making her work as their slave, a plot based on the real-life Elizabeth Canning case of 1753–54. The story conforms more closely to the conventional mystery, although there is no murder. A local solicitor, who is consulted by the women, is convinced of their innocence and sets out to prove it. The mystery is, of course, centred on the girl. If her story is false from start to finish, how did she obtain the facts which enabled her to lie so convincingly? An uncomplicated structure and the first-person narrative—the tale is told by the solicitor—engage the reader both with the characters, who are exceptionally well drawn, and with the social and class prejudices of the small-town community—prejudices which the author to some extent undoubtedly shared.

Josephine Tey not only has retained her hold on readers of detective fiction, but is now being resurrected in the novels of Nicola Upson, who sets her mysteries in the years between the wars and peoples them with real-life characters of the time, Josephine Tey being her serial protagonist. Famous detectives have from time to time been resurrected on film or in print—Jill Paton Walsh is continuing the Wimsey saga—but Nicola Upson is the first writer to choose a previous real-life crime novelist as an ongoing character.

The great majority of detectives in the Golden Age were men—and, indeed, if they were professional police officers, had to be male, since women at that time had a very limited role in policing. In general women characters who dabbled in detection were either sidekicks or cheerful crusaders-in-arms to the dominant male hero, serving as either a Watson or a love interest, or both. One obvious exception is Agatha Christie's Miss Marple, who is not only unique in working entirely alone, without the help of a Watson, but in being invariably cleverer than the police detectives she encounters, and whose sex life, if any, is mercifully shrouded in mystery. But as time progressed it was thought necessary that even the women who played a subsidiary part in the triumphs of the male hero should have some kind of job in their own right rather than sit at home ministering to the needs of their spouse. In the Campion novels by Margery Allingham, Lady Amanda Fitton, who finally marries Albert Campion and who, if the author's hints are to be believed, presumably becomes at least a viscountess, is blessed not only with a title of her own, but with a job as an aircraft designer—although we never hear her discussing her job, nor is she ever seen at her drawing board. Lord Peter Wimsey's

Harriet Vane is a successful novelist, as was the author, but in the four murder investigations in which she features it is Wimsey who plays the dominant part. In *Strong Poison* he saves her from execution, and in *Have His Carcase*, the novel in which Harriet discovers the bloodless body on Flat Iron Rock, he arrives, partly because he can't resist the challenge of a corpse, but principally to save Harriet from the embarrassment of being regarded as a suspect. In *Gaudy Night* Harriet actually calls him in to investigate a mystery which she should have been able to solve herself if her mind hadn't been preoccupied with the difficulty for a woman of reconciling the emotional and intellectual life, and in particular her own relationship with Lord Peter. Georgia Cavendish, the wife of Nicholas Blake's hero Nigel Strangeways, is a celebrated traveller and explorer with a flamboyant taste in fashion and a highly original and strong personality. It is interesting that neither Harriet Vane nor Georgia Cavendish is described as beautiful although both, particularly Georgia, are sexually attractive, and so of course is Lady Amanda.

Although women detectives play little part in the novels of the Golden Age, somewhat surprisingly they appeared very early in the history of crime writing. To discuss their exploits and examine their significance to the genre requires a whole book—which has, indeed, been written by Patricia Craig and Mary Cadogan in their fascinating *The Lady Investigates* (1981). I am particularly sorry not to have encountered Lady Molly of Scotland Yard, the creation of Baroness Orczy, more famous for the Scarlet Pimpernel stories. The majority of Baroness Orczy's detective stories were written before the full flowering of the Golden Age, but in 1925 she published *Unravelled Knots*, which foreshadowed later English armchair detectives who, physically disabled and unable to sally forth, solved crimes by a mixture of intuition and clues brought to them by a peripatetic colleague, of which Josephine Tey's *The Daughter of Time* is probably the best-known English example. Lady Molly appeared in 1910 and one can only agree with the "high-born Frenchwoman" who describes her as "a true-hearted English woman, the finest product on God's earth, after all's said and done." Baroness Orczy was probably aware that none of her readers in 1910 would think that consorting with the police in a criminal investigation was a proper job for a lady, even for a true-hearted English woman, but Lady Molly, like others of her time, is sacrificing herself to vindicate her husband, who is languishing in Dartmoor prison, wrongly convicted of murder. Needless to say, Scotland Yard officers are at Lady Molly's feet and adulation is inspired in everyone she encounters. The story is told by her sidekick, Mary Granard, who used to be her maid and who idolises her dear lady's beauty, charm, brains and style, and the marvellous intuition which, in Mary's opinion, made her the most wonderful psychologist of her time. The relationship between them is one of sickening sentimentality. Mary, who obviously serves the function of a Watson, complained while on a case that there was something she didn't understand. " 'No, and you won't until we get there,' Lady Molly replied, running up to me and kissing me in her pretty engaging way." I suspect that Lady Molly's husband was in no hurry to be liberated from Dartmoor prison.

Not surprisingly, given the talents of many of the writers, the Golden Age detective stories were competently and sometimes very well written, and some of the best will endure. Nevertheless, subtlety of characterisation, a setting which came alive for the reader and credibility of motive were often subjugated, particularly in the humdrums, to the demand to provide an intriguing and mysterious plot. Writers vied with each other in their search for an original method of murder and for clues of increasing ingenuity and complexity. Webster has written that death has ten thousand doors to let out life, and it seems that most of them have at one time or another been used. Unfortunate victims were despatched by licking poisoned stamps, being battered to death by church bells, stunned by a falling pot, stabbed with an icicle, poisoned by cat claws and not infrequently found dead in locked and barred rooms with looks of appalling terror on their faces. This world was summed up by William Trevor, the Anglo-Irish novelist and short story writer, when he spoke of reading detective stories as a child in his acceptance speech on winning a literary award in 1999.

> All over England, it seemed to me, bodies were being discovered by housemaids in libraries. Village poison pens were tirelessly at work. There was murder in Mayfair, on trains, in airships, in Palm Court lounges, between the acts. Golfers stumbled over corpses on fairways. Chief Constables awoke to them in their gardens.
>
> We had nothing like it in West Cork.

Nor in West Kensington either.

These novels are, of course, paradoxical. They deal with violent death and violent emotions, but they are novels of escape. We are required to feel no real pity for the victim, no empathy for the murderer, no sympathy for the falsely accused. For whomever the bell tolls, it doesn't toll for us. Whatever our secret terrors, we are not the body on the library floor. And in the end, by the grace of Poirot's little grey cells, all will be well— except of course with the murderer, but he deserves all that's coming to him. All the mysteries will be explained, all the problems solved, and peace and order will return to that mythical village which, despite its above-average homicide rate, never really loses its tranquillity or its innocence. Rereading the Golden Age novels with their confident morality, their lack of any empathy with the murderer and the popularity of their rural settings, readers can still enter nostalgically this settled and comfortable world. "Stands the church clock at ten to three?" And is there arsenic still for tea?

It was a tough case. Plenty of witnesses,
but no one was talking.

4

Soft-centred and Hard-boiled

> It was about eleven o'clock in the morning, mid-
> October, with the sun not shining and a look of
> hard wet rain in the clearness of the foothills. . . . I
> was neat, clean, shaved and sober, and I didn't care
> who knew it. I was everything the well-dressed pri-
> vate detective ought to be. I was calling on four
> million dollars.
>
> *Raymond Chandler,* The Big Sleep

WHILE THE well-born and impeccably correct detectives of the Golden Age were courteously interviewing their suspects in the drawing rooms of country houses, the studies of rural clergymen and the rooms of Oxford academics, across the Atlantic crime writers were finding their material and inspiration in a very different society and writing about it in prose that was colloquial, vivid and memorable. Although this book is primarily about British detective novelists, the commonly described hard-boiled school of American fiction, rooted in a different continent and in a different literary tradition, has made such an important contribution to crime writing that to ignore its achievements would be seriously misleading. The two most famous innovators, Dashiell Hammett and Raymond Chandler, have had a lasting influence beyond the crime genre, both in their own country and abroad.

No writer, whatever form his fiction takes, can distance himself entirely from the country, civilisation and century of which he is a part. A reader coming from Dashiell Hammett or Raymond Chandler to Agatha Christie or Dorothy L. Sayers could reasonably feel that these writers were living not only on different continents but in different centuries. So what England were these predominantly middle-class, well-educated novelists and their devoted readers portraying, what traditions, beliefs and prejudices were the purveyors of popular literature consciously or unconsciously reflecting?

As I was born in 1920 it was an England I knew, a cohesive world, overwhelmingly white and united by a common belief in a religious and moral code based on the Judeo-Christian inheritance—even if this belief was not invariably reflected in practice—and buttressed by social and political institutions which, although they might be criticised, attracted general allegiance, and were accepted as necessary to the well-being of the state: the monarchy, the Empire, the Church, the criminal justice system, the City, the ancient universities. It was an ordered society in which virtue was regarded as normal, crime an aberration, and in which there was small sympathy for the criminal; it was generally accepted that murderers, when convicted, would hang— although Agatha Christie, arch-purveyor of cosy reassurance, is careful not to emphasise this disagreeable fact or allow the dark shadow of the public hangman to fall upon her essentially comfortable pages. The death penalty is mentioned by Margery Allingham, and Dorothy L. Sayers in *Busman's Honeymoon* actually has the temerity to confront Lord Peter Wimsey with the logical end to his detective activities, when he crouches weeping in his wife's arms on the morning when Frank Crutchley hangs. Some readers may feel that, if he couldn't face the inevitable outcome of his detective hobby, he should have confined himself to collecting first editions.

Despite the turbulent antagonisms of postwar Europe and the growth of fascism, the 1930s were years of remarkable freedom from domestic crime, and although there must have been areas, particularly of the inner cities, which were at least as violent as they are today, pictures of this disruption were not being brought daily into people's sitting-rooms by television and the Internet. It was therefore possible to live in a country town or in a village and feel almost entirely secure. We can read an Agatha Christie novel set in what seems a mythical village, in which the inhabitants are happily reconciled to their allotted rank and station, and we feel that this is an exaggerated, romanticised or idealised world. It isn't, not altogether. Dorothy L. Sayers describes it in *Busman's Honeymoon*. Harriet is speaking of her husband, Lord Peter:

> She understood now why it was that, with all his masking attitudes . . . he yet carried about with him that permanent atmosphere of security. He belonged to an ordered society and this was it. More than any of the friends in her own world he spoke the familiar language of her childhood. In London anybody at any moment might do or become anything, but in a village, no matter what village, they were all immutably themselves, parson, organist,

sweep, duke's son and doctor's daughter, moving like chessmen upon their allotted squares.

It is precisely this view of England that in general the 1930s' detective writers, particularly women, were portraying: middle-class, hierarchical, rural, peaceable. But it was an age of underlying anxiety. Before the institution of the welfare state, the dread of unemployment, of sickness, of economic failure was very real, and the growing power of the fascist dictators abroad threatened the possibility of a further war before the country had recovered from the appalling carnage, social upheaval and personal tragedies of the 1914–18 conflict. Already the posturing of home-grown fascism was provoking violent clashes, particularly in London's East End. It was small wonder that people longed for that "permanent atmosphere of security" and were able to find it, at least temporarily, in a popular form which was both ordered and reassuring.

The differences between the hard-boiled school and such Golden Age writers as Agatha Christie, Dorothy L. Sayers and Michael Innes, are so profound that it seems stretching a definition to describe both groups under the same category. If the British detective story is concerned with bringing order out of disorder, a genre of reconciliation and social healing, restoring the mythical village of Mayhem Parva to prelapsarian tranquillity, in the United States Hammett and Chandler were depicting and exploring the great social upheavals of the 1920s—lawlessness, prohibition, corruption, the power and violence of notorious gangsters who were close to becoming folk heroes, the cycle of boom and depression—and creating detectives who were inured to this world and could confront it on their own terms.

Dashiell Hammett (1894–1961) had a tough and underprivileged youth working on the railway, then as a Pinkerton detective, and as a soldier in the First World War. He was discharged as tubercular, married his hospital nurse and had two children, supporting his family by writing short stories for the pulp magazines that were extremely popular during the 1920s. The editors demanded violent action, vividly portrayed characters and a prose style ruthlessly pruned of all inessentials; all this Hammett provided.

Hammett's stories are not about restoring the moral order, nor are they set in a world in which the problem of evil can be solved by Poirot's little grey cells or Miss Marple's cosy homilies, a world as innocuous as flower-arranging. Hammett knew from traumatic personal experience how precarious is the moral tightrope which the private investigator daily walks in his battle with the criminal. The first of his detectives has worked for fifteen years as an operative for the Continental Detective Agency and is known only as "Continental Op." It is appropriate that the Op is unnamed. There is nothing subtle about him and little we expect to know—except his age, thirty-five, that he is short and fat, and that his only loyalty is to the Continental Detective Agency and his job. But there is an honesty and directness about this personal code, limited as it may be.

> "I like being a detective, like the work. And liking work makes you want to do it as well as you can. Otherwise there'd be no sense to it."

The Op tells his own story, but flatly, without explanations, excuses or embellishments. He is as ruthless as the world in which he operates, a violent gun-carrying dispenser of the only justice he recognises. Short and fat he may be, but in *Red Harvest* (1929) he takes on the combined strength of the police, corrupt politicians and gangsters to cleanse the city of Personville, meeting violence with violence. His loyalty to the job means that he doesn't take bribes; indeed he seems impervious to the lure of money—in this, at least, he is superior to the company he keeps. He is naturally solitary, and how could he be otherwise with such a job in a corrupt and lawless world? When a woman attempts to seduce him, his response is a brutal rejection; later, to get rid of her, he shoots her in the leg, but not without a certain compunction: "I had never shot a woman before. I felt queer about it." There is not much that the Op feels queer about.

Hammett's most famous detective, Sam Spade, whose hunting-ground is San Francisco, appears only in one full-length novel, *The Maltese Falcon* (1930), but this book, his best known, and the film in which Humphrey Bogart portrayed the detective, have ensured that Spade has become the archetypical hard-boiled private eye. Like the Op, Spade's only loyalty is to his work and to his colleagues. He is classless, younger and more physically attractive than the Op, but there is a cruelty in his ruthlessness and he is the more immoral of the two, capable of falling in love with a woman but never putting love above the demands of the job.

After the success of *The Maltese Falcon*, Hammett was offered a job as a screenwriter in Hollywood. There he met the playwright Lillian Hellman and began a love affair which lasted until his death. After this move to the highly lucrative and hedonistic world of Hollywood, he began drinking heavily and lived in a way which a friend described as making sense "only if he had no expectations of being alive much beyond Thursday." During the Hollywood years he became involved with left-wing political causes and in 1951 was sentenced to six months in prison because he would not give evidence against Communists who had jumped bail. After his release his books were proscribed, and during his final ten years he lived on the charity of others. He would not be the only writer whose talent was destroyed by money, self-indulgence and the egregious temptations of fame, but perhaps for him the temptations were the more irresistible because of the penury and struggles of those early years.

Might Hammett have written another novel as good as *The Maltese Falcon* if he had resisted that invitation to move to Hollywood? I think it doubtful. It may be that by then he had said all he wanted to and that his talent was exhausted. Nevertheless, his achievement remains remarkable. In a writing career of little more than a decade he raised a commonly despised genre into writing which had a valid claim to be taken seriously as literature. He showed crime writers that what is important goes beyond an ingenious plot, mystery and suspense. More important are the novelist's individual voice, the reality of the world he creates and the strength and originality of the writing.

The early life of Raymond Chandler, born in 1888, was markedly different from that of Hammett. He was educated in England at Dulwich College and returned to the United States in 1912, where he had a successful business career before retiring in 1933 to devote himself to writing. Like Hammett, he learned his craft by contributing to the pulp magazines but wrote later that he rejected the editor's insistence in cutting out all descriptions on the grounds that the readers disliked anything that held up the action.

> I set out to prove them wrong. My theory was that the readers just *thought* they cared about nothing but the action; that really, although they didn't know it, the thing they cared about, and that I cared about, was the creation of emotion through dialogue and description.

And that was what, superbly, Chandler provided. In this he reminds me of a very different writer but one who was also brilliant at writing dialogue, Evelyn Waugh. When asked why he never described what his characters were thinking, Waugh replied that he didn't know what they were thinking, he only knew what they said and did. The hard-boiled detectives are not introspective; it is through action and dialogue that their story is told.

Chandler's hero, Philip Marlowe, accepts that he is earning a precarious and dangerous living in a world which is lawless, tawdry and corrupt but, unlike Spade, he has a social conscience, personal integrity and a moral code beyond unquestioning loyalty to his job and colleagues. He is discriminating about the kind of work he will accept, never takes tainted money or betrays a friend, and is totally loyal even to undeserving clients. More personally vulnerable than Spade, he is a more reluctant private eye, troubled and repelled by the corrupt and heartless world in which he earns his living and uncomfortably sensitive to the suffering of its victims. In the words of a character in *The Long Goodbye*,

"There ain't no clean way to make a hundred million bucks. . . . Somewhere along

the line guys got pushed to the wall, nice
little businesses got the ground cut out
from under them. . . . Decent people lost
their jobs. . . . Big money is big power and
big power gets used wrong. It's the system."

Marlowe tells his story in the first person in prose
that is terse but richly descriptive and larded with
wisecracks.

I wasn't wearing a gun. . . . I doubted if it
would do me any good. The big man
would probably take it away from me and
eat it.

The story may at times be incoherent but the
writing never disappoints in what Chandler cared
most about, the creation of emotion through dialogue and description.

Both Sam Spade and Philip Marlowe are
licensed investigators and, unlike the British amateur detectives, have to some extent a recognised
function and authority. But their attitude to
the police is ambivalent, ranging from a wary and
reluctant co-operation to open enmity. The police are seen by both as brutal and corrupt. Captain Gregorius of *The Long Goodbye* "solves

crimes with the bright light, the soft sap, the kick to the kidneys, the knee to the groin, the fist to the solar plexus, the night stick to the base of the spine." Even after a beating from Gregorius, Marlowe, unyielding to his brutality, has the courage to hurl his contempt in Gregorius's face. "I wouldn't betray an enemy into your hands. You're not only a gorilla, you're an incompetent." How different from the honest and paternal Superintendent Kirk in Dorothy L. Sayers's *Busman's Honeymoon*, unable to speak grammatical English when discussing the case of the body in the cellar with Peter Wimsey, but always ready to compete with Lord Peter in dredging up an appropriate quotation to demonstrate his literary credentials.

In a famous passage from his critical essay *The Simple Art of Murder*, Chandler describes his detective in words which were more appropriate to a work of high romance:

In everything that can be called art there is a quality of redemption. . . . But down these mean streets a man must go who is not himself mean, who is neither tarnished nor afraid. The detective in this kind of story must be such a man. He is the hero, he is everything. . . . He must be the best man in his world and a good enough man for any world.

This is surely too romantic and unrealistic a view to be credible. The vision of Continental Op, Sam Spade, or even the compassionate Marlowe, riding forth like a knight errant to redress the evils of the world of which he is a part, does violence both to the ethos of the hard-boiled school and to the character, and surely makes Marlowe as much a figure of fantasy as Lord Peter Wimsey.

Very different, too, is the hard-boiled detectives' response to women. The Op and Spade generally preserve their emotions as inviolate as the secrets they uncover, and only Marlowe is susceptible to love. Here are no brave and cheerful comrades-in-arms, no devoted non-interfering wives at home with their knitting, no successful professional women with interesting lives of their own, no carefully crafted figures of wish-fulfilment. The women in the hard-boiler are sexually alluring temptresses seen by the hero as inimical both to their masculine code and to the success of the job. They may not all get shot in the leg, but if guilty they are likely to be handed over to the police without compunction.

We have, of course, always had the most notable detective stories of America and Canada available in this country, including the hard-boiled school. I came to the American hard-boiled school in the 1960s through the work of Ross Macdonald, the pseudonym of Kenneth Millar (1915–1983), and he remains my favourite of the triumvirate of the best-known hard-boiled writers. His childhood was a tragic odyssey of poverty and rejection. His mother, deserted by her husband when Macdonald was three, dragged him round Canada depending on the charity of relatives, and Macdonald narrowly escaped the appalling fate of being consigned to an orphanage. Such pain in childhood is never forgotten and seldom forgiven, and all his writing life Macdonald's fiction was influenced by the inescapable heritage of the past. His detective, Lew Archer, is in the tradition of Philip Marlowe and, like Marlowe, he casts a critical eye on society, concerned particularly with the searing damage to the human spirit caused by the ruthlessness, greed and corruption of big business. Although Macdonald's complicated plots are not without violence, he is more a detached observer than a participator, somewhat resembling a secular Father Brown in his empathy for human suffering. Less romantic than Chandler, his style has the vigour and imaginative richness of a man confident of his mastery of epithets and, particularly in his later novels, he attains a standard which places him first among those novelists who raised the genre from its roots in pulp fiction to serious literature. In an influential review in 1969, the writer Eudora Welty described his work as "the finest series of detective novels ever written by an American," a verdict with which I feel few critics would disagree.

For me the most remarkable of the moderns is Sara Paretsky. When she created her private eye, V. I. Warshawski, it was in conscious emulation of the myth of the solitary private eye and his lone campaign against the corruption of the powerful, but her Polish-American heroine has a humility, a humanity and a need for human relationships which the male hard-boilers lack. Her territory is Chicago, not the Chicago of the dramatic city centre or the prosperous suburbs, but the city's southeast side, the neighbourhood of the poor who live in shanties on the contaminated marshland known as Dead Stick Pond. Paretsky creates a powerful vision of the Chicago where V. I. Warshawski grew up and where she operates as a courageous, sexually liberated female investigator. Through her heroine and in her private life of speaking and journalism, Paretsky conducts her campaign against injustice and, in particular, for the right of women to control their lives and their sexuality. No other female crime writer has so powerfully and effectively combined a well-crafted detective story with the novel of social realism and protest. And here, too, we see the influence of Raymond Chandler.

Chandler despised the English school of crime writing, stating that "the English may not always be the best writers in the world, but they are incomparably the best dull writers," his most vituperative criticism being directed at Dorothy L. Sayers. In 1930, the year in which Hammett published *The Maltese Falcon*, the Golden Age in England was at the height of its popularity. Agatha Christie brought out *The Murder at the Vicarage*, Dorothy L. Sayers *Strong Poison*, Margery Allingham *Mystery Mile*, and, four years later, Ngaio Marsh was to make her debut with *A Man Lay Dead*. These four highly successful women are among the relatively few whose books are still in print and read today, a longevity undoubtedly sustained, in the case of Christie and Sayers, by television. All four consolidated and affirmed the structure and conventions of the classical detective story, inventing detectives who have entered into the mythology of the genre. Three of the women aspired to, and achieved, a standard of writing and characterisation which helped to raise the reputation of the detective story from a harmless but predictable literary diversion into a popular form that could be taken as seriously as a well-written mainstream novel.

For me they have an additional interest. To read the detective novels of these four women is to learn more about the England in which they lived and worked than most popular social histories can provide, and in particular about the status of women in the years between the wars. For this reason, if no other, they should have a chapter to themselves.

5

Four Formidable Women

Agatha's best work is, like P. G. Wodehouse and
Noel Coward's best work, the most characteristic
pleasure-writing of this epoch and will appear one
day in all decent literary histories. As *writing* it is
not distinguished, but as *story* it is superb.

Robert Graves, letter, 15 July 1944

REAMS OF paper have been expended on
attempts to explore the secret of Agatha
Christie's success. Writers who explore
the phenomenon not uncommonly begin with
the arithmetic of her achievements: outsold only
by the Bible and Shakespeare, translated into over
one hundred foreign languages, author of the
longest-running play ever seen on the London
stage and, in addition, recipient of awards that
success usually affords only to the highest literary
talent—a Dame of the British Empire and an
honorary degree of Doctor of Literature from
Oxford University. The perennial question re-

"Check with our legal people if we can publish a detective story in which the murderer turns out to be the author."

mains, how did this gently reared, essentially Edwardian lady do it?

Certainly Christie's universal appeal doesn't lie in blood or violence. Not for her the bullet-ridden corpses down Raymond Chandler's mean city streets, the urban jungle of the wisecracking, fast-shooting, sardonic private eye or the careful psychological examination of human depravity. Although both her best-known detectives, Poirot and Miss Marple, occasionally investigated murder overseas, her natural world as perceived by her readers is a romanticised cosy English village rooted in nostalgia, with its ordered hierarchy: the wealthy squire (often with a new young wife of mysterious antecedence), the retired irascible colonel, the village doctor and the district nurse, the chemist (useful for the purchase of poison), the gossiping spinsters behind their lace curtains, the parson in his vicarage, all moving predictably in their social hierarchy like pieces on a chessboard. Her style is neither original nor elegant but it is workmanlike. It does what is required of it. She employs no great psychological subtlety in her characterisation; her villains and suspects are drawn in broad and clear outlines and, perhaps because of this, they have a universality which readers worldwide can instantly recognise and feel at home with. Above all she is a literary conjuror who places her pasteboard characters face downwards and shuffles them with practised cunning. Game after game we are confident that this time we will turn up the card with the face of the true murderer, and time after time she defeats us. And with a Christie mystery no suspect can safely be eliminated, even the narrator of the story. With other mystery writers of the Golden Age we can be reasonably confident that the murderer won't be one of the attractive young lovers, a policeman, a servant or a child, but Agatha Christie has no favourites with either murderer or victim. Most mystery writers jib, as do I, at killing the very young, but Agatha Christie is tough, as ready to murder a child, admittedly a precocious unappealing one, as she is to despatch a blackmailer. With Mrs. Christie, as with real life, the only certainty is death.

Perhaps her greatest strength was that she never overstepped the limits of her talent. She knew precisely what she could do and she did it well. For over fifty years this shy and conventional woman produced murder mysteries of extraordinarily imaginative duplicity. With her immense output the quality is inevitably uneven—some of the later books in particular show a sad falling-off—but at her best the ingenuity is dazzling. Her prime skill as a storyteller is the talent to deceive, and it is possible to identify some of the tricks, often verbal, by which she gently seduces us into self-deception. In time we almost match the cunning of the author. We beware of entering that most lethal of rooms, the country house library, we become suspicious of the engaging ne'er-do-well returning from foreign parts and take careful note of mirrors, twins and androgynous names. She is particularly fond of a version of the eternal triangle in which a couple, apparently happily engaged or married, are menaced by a third person, sometimes predatory and rich. When the victim is murdered there is little mystery about the chief suspect. Only at the end of the book does Miss Christie turn the triangle round and we recognise that it was that way up all the time. And her clues are brilliantly designed to confuse. The butler goes over to peer closely at a calendar. She has planted in our mind the suspicion that a crucial clue relates to dates and times, but the clue is, in fact, that the butler is short-sighted.

Both the trickery and the final solution are invariably more ingenious than believable. The books are mild intellectual puzzles, not credible blueprints for real murder. In *Death on the Nile*, for example, the murderer is required to dash round the deck of a crowded river-steamer, acting with split-second precision and depending on not being observed either by passengers or by crew. In another book we are told that the murderer unscrews the digits of a number on the door of a hostel room, so luring the victim to the wrong room. In real life we never go unerringly to the room we want; we identify it by the floor and by the numbers on adjoining doors. In *Dumb Witness* the clue is that a brooch made of initials is glimpsed in a mirror at night. But the brooch is worn by a woman in a dressing-gown—the last garment on which a heavy brooch would normally be pinned. But to the Christie aficionado this is mere quibbling. And indeed it does seem ungracious to point out inconsistencies or incredulities in books which are primarily intended to entertain—a far from ignoble aim—and in which the reader is in general treated fairly and falls more often than not into a pit of his own devising.

The moral basis of the books is unambiguous and simple, epitomised by Poirot's declaration: "I have a bourgeois attitude to murder: I disapprove of it." But even the horror of murder is sanitised;

the necessary violence is perfunctorily described, there is no grief, no loss, an absence of outrage. We feel that at the end of the book the victim will get up, wipe off the artificial blood and be restored to life. The last thing we get from a Christie novel is the disturbing presence of evil. Admittedly Poirot and Miss Marple occasionally used the word, but with no more relevance than if they were referring to the smell of bad drains. One of the secrets of her universal and enduring appeal is that it excludes all disturbing emotions; those are for the real world from which we are escaping, not for St. Mary Mead. All the problems and uncertainties of life are subsumed in the one central problem: the identity of the killer. And we know that, by the end of the book, this will be satisfactorily solved and peace and order restored to that mythical village whose inhabitants, apparently so harmless and familiar, prove so enigmatic, so surprising in their ingenious villainy.

Agatha Christie hasn't in my view had a profound influence on the later development of the detective story. She wasn't an innovative writer and had no interest in exploring the possibilities of the genre. What she consistently provided is a strong and exciting narrative, the challenge of a puzzle, an accommodating and accessible style and original detectives in Poirot and Miss Marple, whom readers can encounter in book after book with the comfortable assurance that they are meeting old friends. Her main influence on contemporary crime writers was to affirm the popularity and importance of ingenuity in clue plotting and of surprise in the final solution, thus helping significantly to set the limited range and the conventions of what were to become the books of the Golden Age. Dorothy L. Sayers could have been thinking of Agatha Christie when she wrote:

> Just at present . . . the fashion in detective fiction is to have characters credible and lively; not conventional but, on the other hand, not too profoundly studied—people who live more or less on the *Punch* level of emotion.

It seems a little unjust to classify Agatha Christie's characters as being on the *Punch* level. She is more than that. She may draw them in clear outline with none of the ambiguities of shading, but she gives us enough to enable us to feel that we know them. But do we? Are they, like the material clues, intended to deceive?

Rereading a selection of her stories to affirm or modify my existing prejudices I found some had lost even their ability to keep me reading. Others surprised me by being both better written and more ingeniously puzzling than I had remembered, among them one published in 1950, *A Murder Is Announced*. For me, this story demonstrates both her strength and her weakness. Here we have the usual village setting, Chipping Cleghorn, and a cast of characters typical of Christieland, but the setting is described with more realism than in the later books, and a keener eye to the economic changes and social nuances brought about by the difficult post-war years. As usual with Christie the dialogue is particularly effective, but here it is used not merely to reveal character but to contain vital clues, one of which even the most careful reader would probably miss. The people are drawn with economy but with more subtlety than usual, and both the motive for the murders and the solution to the mystery derive directly from the characters, their unchangeable past and living present. This ability to fuse character with clues is one of the marks of a good detective story. Admittedly the end of the novel is disappointing, with over-complicated and contrived relationships and a surfeit of incredible killings. And she was over-fond of the unconvincing contrivance whereby one of the characters acts as a decoy and is on the point of being killed when the police and Miss Marple dash in to arrest the murderer. But in Chipping Cleghorn or St. Mary Mead murder is only a temporary embarrassment. The vicar may find a body on his study floor but it is unlikely to interfere with the preparation of the Sunday sermon. We enter this peaceable and nostalgic world with the confident expectation of taking comfort from Miss Marple's common sense and her enigmatic comments on the crime as we move together to a satisfactory solution in the final chapter, when truth and justice will once more prevail.

And while highly regarded and prizewinning novels of the post-war era are often no longer obtainable, Agatha Christie's books are still ranged on the shelves of bookshops and libraries. Poirot and Miss Marple still appear regularly on our television screens and it is a safe bet that, whenever detection fiction is discussed, the name of Agatha Christie will be mentioned either in praise or in disparagement. Her critics sometimes exhibit vehemence close to personal outrage, seeing her books as trivial, intellectually feeble and written without distinction of style or subtlety of characterisation. But one thing is certain: Agatha Christie has provided entertainment, suspense and temporary relief from the anxieties and traumas of life in both peace and war for millions throughout the world and this is an achievement which merits our gratitude and respect. I suspect that a traveller, stranded in an airport hotel overnight and finding in the bedside cabinet two novels, the latest winner of a prestigious literary prize and an Agatha Christie, would reach for the latter to assuage the half-acknowledged fear of contemporary travel and the discomfort and boredom of a long night.

Of the four women writers I have chosen to illustrate detective stories as social history, Dorothy L. Sayers, who was born in 1893 and died in 1957, was the most versatile: novelist, poet, playwright, amateur theologian, Christian apologist, translator of Dante. It is a safe assumption that any aficionado of the classical detective story, asked to name the six best writers in the genre, would include her name. Yet paradoxically there is no other writer of the Golden Age who provokes such strong and often opposing responses. To her admirers she is the writer who did more than any other to make the detective story intellectually respectable, and to change it from an ingenious but lifeless sub-literary puzzle into a specialised branch of fiction with serious claims to be judged as a novel. To her detractors she is outrageously snobbish, intellectually arrogant, pretentious and occasionally dull. But there can be no doubt of her influence both on succeeding writers and on the genre itself. And she brought to the detective story writing that was always good and scholarly, and occasionally—as in the description of the storm in *The Nine Tailors*—outstanding. Sayers wrote with intelligence, wit, humour, and she created in Lord Peter Wimsey a genuine folk hero whose vitality has ensured his survival. Readers who dislike her novels tend to concentrate their criticism on Lord Peter, finding him snobbish, unconvincing and irritating. But it is apparent that Sayers, who took an ironic and detached view of her creation, had her reading public very much in mind. Writing later to her American publishers, she told them that she would give him "an attractive mother to whom he was much attached, and an immaculate 'gentleman's gentleman'—Bunter by name." Going on, she wrote:

Lord Peter's large income (the source of which, by the way, I have never investigated) was a different matter. I deliberately gave him that. After all, it cost me nothing, and at that time I was particularly hard up and it gave me pleasure to spend his fortune for him. When I was dissatisfied with my single unfurnished room, I took a luxurious flat for him in Piccadilly. When my cheap rug got a hole in it, I ordered an Aubusson carpet. When I had no money to pay my bus fare, I presented him with a Daimler double-six, upholstered in a style of sober magnificence, and when I felt dull I let him drive it.

It was a vicarious satisfaction in the privileges and pleasures of wealth which she could be confident her readers would share.

There is one way in which Dorothy L. Sayers was very much a writer of her own time, and that is the ingenuity of her complicated methods of death. This is one aspect of her talent which has had little influence on modern novelists, and one which we have largely outgrown. Realism and credibility have supplanted ingenuity. Despite her highly original talent and the quality of her writing, she was an innovator of style but not of form, and was content to work within the contemporary conventions of the detective story which in the Golden Age were imperatives. Readers of the 1930s expected that the puzzle would be both dominant and ingenious, and that the murderer in his villainy would exhibit almost superhuman cunning and skill. It was not sufficient that the victim should be murdered; he must be ingeniously, bizarrely and horribly murdered. Those were not the days of the swift bash to the skull followed by sixty thousand words of psychological insight. Because of this need to provide a plot that was both original and ingenious, many of the murders she devised would not have worked in practice. That does not spoil our present-day pleasure in the books, but marks them as very much of their age. *Have His Carcase*, for example, is extraordinarily complex, involving a cipher, letters posted abroad, complicated alibis and unconvincing disguises. It is hard to reconcile this ingenuity with a murderer who is shown as both stupid and brutal, even if he is given a somewhat unlikely accomplice. And how extraordinary that the victim could be a haemophiliac without his doctor, his dentist, the police surgeon or the pathologist noticing the fact within the first few minutes of the post-mortem examination. But was one ever held?

The murder in *Unnatural Death* is equally implausible. It is not really possible to kill someone by injecting air into a vein, at least not with a normal-sized syringe. I am advised that the syringe would have to be so large that the patient would be more likely to die of shock on beholding it than from any effects of the injected air! It is unlikely too that the victim in *The Nine Tailors* would be killed merely by the clanging of bells, however long, loud and close the peal. And I personally could have advised Mr. Tallboy in *Murder Must Advertise* of many simpler and surer ways of killing his blackmailer than by climbing onto the roof and using a catapult through the skylight. Today, in choosing how to despatch our victims, we are less concerned with originality and ingenuity than with practical, scientific and psychological credibility.

But one way in which I suggest that Dorothy L. Sayers was in advance of her age is the realism with which she describes the finding of the body. She well knew the importance of this moment of high drama and she was not too squeamish to show us something of the horror of violent death. In this she was very different from her co-crime-writer Agatha Christie, who obviously felt a deep repugnance for describing physical violence. One cannot imagine Agatha Christie describing with such realism the finding by Harriet Vane of the body with its throat cut on the Flat-Iron Rock.

It *was* a corpse. Not the sort of corpse there could be any doubt about, either . . . Indeed, if the head did not come off in Harriet's hands, it was only because the spine was intact, for the larynx and all the great vessels of the neck had been severed and a frightful stream, bright red and glistening, was running over the surface of the rock and dripping into a little hollow below.

Harriet put the head down again and felt suddenly sick. She had written often enough about this kind of corpse, but meeting the real thing in the flesh was quite different. She had not realised how butcherly the severed vessels would look, and she had not reckoned with the horrid halitus of blood, which steamed to her nostrils under the blazing sun.

To the thirties' writer of detective fiction death was, of course, necessary but, however ingenious or bloody, it was rarely allowed to horrify or distress. Today—and I suggest that Dorothy L.

Sayers had a potent, and perhaps unacknowledged, influence—we aim for greater realism. Murder, the contaminating and unique crime, is messy, horrifying and tragic, and the modern reader of crime fiction is not spared these realities.

But in the more minor expediencies of murder Sayers was typical of her time. She had a liking for maps, rough illustrative drawings, ciphers and house plans. A plan which particularly intrigues me is provided in *Clouds of Witness*, where victim and suspects are guests of the Duke of Denver at his Yorkshire shooting box, Riddlesdale Lodge. A plan of the second floor shows that eight people had to make do with one small bathroom and separate lavatory, a lack which may partly explain the English obsession with the state of their bowels.

For many of Dorothy L. Sayers's readers, perhaps for most, *Gaudy Night* stands at the peak of her artistic achievement. It is unique among her novels—and rare among detective stories—in not having a mysterious death at its heart. There are, of course, two attempted murders, one of the over-sensitive student Miss Newland and one of Harriet Vane herself. The criticism made at the time by female academics was that the novel was out of date, portraying the Oxford not of the thirties, but of Sayers's own student days. The women's college she describes with such loving recollection, with its rigid segregation of the sexes and its formal manners, is, of course, one that has passed away for ever. What relevance has the novel, therefore, for the reader of today and for today's writer of detective fiction?

For me *Gaudy Night* is one of the most successful marriages of the puzzle with the novel of social realism and serious purpose. It tells me, as a writer of today, that it is possible to construct a credible and enthralling mystery and marry it successfully to a theme of psychological subtlety, and this is perhaps the most important of Dorothy L. Sayers's legacies to writers and readers. She wrote to her friend Muriel St. Clare Byrne that *Gaudy Night* was not a detective story at all, but a novel of an almost entirely psychological kind with a mild detective interest. But here I must take issue with the author—a presumptuous and perhaps a dangerous thing to do. She did herself less than justice. *Gaudy Night* is a true detective story. We want to know who among a closed circle of suspects is responsible for the malicious disruption at Shrewsbury College, and the clues to the mystery are fairly, indeed plainly, presented. I can still recall my first reading of the novel, when I was sixteen, and my self-disgust at my failure to identify the culprit when all the necessary information had been so carefully, if cunningly, provided.

Margery Allingham also portrayed aspects of the age in which she wrote, but was happy to range outside territory with which she was familiar. *Flowers for the Judge* deals with publishing; *Dancers in Mourning* with the frenetic world of the theatrical star; *The Fashion in Shrouds* with the ephemeral mystique of a high-fashion house. All provide a vivid picture of the community in which they are set. Her writing life was long (forty-five years) and apart from published articles, broadcasts and book reviews, she wrote twenty novels of crime and adventure between 1929 and 1966. The novels became increasingly sophisticated, concentrating more on character and milieu than on mystery, and in 1961 she wrote that the crime novel could be "a kind of reflection on society's conscience." This was to become increasingly true of detective fiction generally, but Allingham herself reflected rather than criticised the age in which her stories are set. She had considerable descriptive gifts, especially for places: the seedier squares of north-west London, decaying post-war streets, the salt marshes of the Essex coast. Like Dorothy L. Sayers, she created an upper-class detective (in Albert Campion)—so grand, apparently, that the name of his mother can only be whispered—but one who developed psychological subtlety and, indeed, even changed his appearance as she found the original Campion inadequate to the widening scope of her creative art.

She is notable too for the creation of eccentrics who never degenerate into caricatures, except perhaps for Magersfontein Lugg, who, despite the occasional usefulness of skills developed in his criminal past, is a little too much the traditional stage comedy cockney to be convincing and who would surely be too unsuitable a manservant for even Campion to tolerate. One of the Allingham novels which, for me, best illustrates her talent is the cleverly named *More Work for the Undertaker* (Allingham was good at choosing titles), published in 1949. In this novel, set in one of the gloomier streets of post-war London, she combined the eccentric Palinode household with a vivid evocation of place and a strong and continually exciting narrative to produce what was recognised at the time as a distinguished detective story.

Ngaio Marsh has justified her own statement that "The mechanics of a detective story may be shamelessly contrived but the writing need not be." It has been said that the formula for a successful detective story is 50 percent good detection, 25 percent character and 25 percent what the writer knows best. Ngaio Marsh, a New Zealander, made good use of her own distinguished career in the theatre by setting some of her most successful books, notably *Enter a Murderer*, *Opening Night* and *Death at the Dolphin*, in the world of drama, making excellent use of backstage intrigue and giving a lively account of the problems and mechanics of running a professional company of players in the years between the wars. She is less concerned with the psychology of her characters than is Margery Allingham, and the lengthy interrogations by her urbane detective, Superintendent Roderick Alleyn, have their longueurs, but both women are novelists, not merely fabricators of ingenious puzzles. Both sought, not always successfully, to reconcile the conventions of the classical detective story with the novel of social realism. But because Ngaio Marsh experienced Britain as a long-staying visitor who saw what she thought of as a second homeland through somewhat naïve and uncritical eyes, she gives a less accurate, more idealised, nostalgic and regrettably sometimes snobbish picture of England than do her crime-writing contemporaries. I have most enjoyed the books set in her native New Zealand, *Vintage Murder* (1937), *Colour Scheme* (1943) and *Died in the Wool* (1945), where landscapes, characters and plot are interrelated and she brings the people and the soil of her native county vividly before us.

None of these women, of course, would have described herself as a social historian or as having a prime responsibility either to portray contemporary mores or to criticise the age in which she worked, and it is perhaps this detachment of purpose which makes these writers so reliable as historians of their age. They were of their time and wrote for their time and their stories give a clear and, indeed, a personal account of what it was like to live and work as an educated woman in the decades between the wars.

The 1914–18 war had, of course, very greatly advanced the cause of women's emancipation. They gained the vote and already had the right to a university education but not to a degree until 1920, when in October of that year Dorothy L. Sayers was one of the first women to receive an Oxford degree. The professions were now open to them, but their lives were still extraordinarily restricted compared with today. The mass slaughter of young men in the Great War had meant that there were three million so-called surplus women and very few opportunities open to them, since married men were given priority for jobs. Dorothy L. Sayers deals with this most tellingly, particularly in her treatment of Miss Climpson and her Cattery, a small group of spinsters employed by Lord Peter to assist his detective work. He explains their function to Inspector Parker in *Unnatural Death*.

Miss Climpson is a manifestation of the wasteful way in which this country is run. Thousands of old maids, simply bursting with useful energy, forced by our stupid social system into hydros and hotels and communities and hostels and posts as companions, where their magnificent gossip-powers and units of inquisitiveness are allowed to dissipate themselves, or even become harmful to the community, while the ratepayer's money is spent on getting work for which these women are providentially fitted, inefficiently carried out by ill-equipped policemen like you.

Dorothy L. Sayers, among much in her books that is tendentious or over-romanticised, does deal realistically with the problem of the so-called superfluous women deprived of the hope of marriage by the slaughter of the 1914–18 war, women with intelligence, initiative and often with education, for whom society offered no real intellectual outlet. And those who did find intellectual satisfaction commonly achieved it at the sacrifice of emotional and sexual fulfilment. It is interesting and, I think, significant that there is no married don in *Gaudy Night* and only one married woman—and she a widow—Mrs. Goodwin, who is a member of the senior common room. Women in the Civil Service and teaching were required to resign on marriage, the supposition obviously being that now they had a man to support them they should direct their energies to the proper sphere of interest for their sex. I cannot think of a single detective story written by a woman in the 1930s which features a woman lawyer, a woman surgeon, a woman politician, or indeed a woman in any real position of political or economic power.

One notable exception to the way in which women were perceived as wives, mothers, useful little helpmeets such as stenographers and secretaries, is Margery Allingham's Lady Amanda Fitton. Another Allingham heroine who has a professional job is Val Ferris, Albert Campion's sister, who has been unhappily married but now works singlemindedly to establish herself as a leading dress designer. She and the actress Georgia are in love with the same man, and the book *The Fashion in Shrouds* explores the emotional pressures on women who dedicate themselves to a career but also want fulfilment in their emotional lives, a problem which is also one of the themes of Dorothy L. Sayers's *Gaudy Night*. Val and Georgia are described in the novel as "two fine ladies of the modern world," but both are aware of their inner dissatisfaction as they drive home alone to their bijoux, hard-earned houses. The novelist says: "Their several responsibilities are far heavier than most men's and their abilities greater," but their femininity—"femininity unprotected from itself"—is presented as "a weakness, not a strength." And when Alan, Val's future husband, proposes to her, he sets out his terms unambiguously. He wants to take "full responsibility" for Val, including financial responsibility, and expects in turn that she will yield to him "your independence, the enthusiasm which you give your career, your time and your thought." She does this almost with a sigh of relief. It is very difficult to imagine a modern writer of detective stories, particularly a woman, thinking that this is a satisfactory solution to Val's dilemma. It is even more difficult to imagine a modern female reader tolerating such blatant misogyny.

Ngaio Marsh is also of her age in the ingenuity of her methods of murder, and surprisingly ruthless and robust in her despatch of victims. In *Died in the Wool*, set in a sheep station, Florence Rubrick is stunned and then suffocated in a bale of wool. The victim in *Off with His Head* is decapitated. In *Scales of Justice*, Colonel Carterette, after being struck on the temple, is killed by the point of a shooting-stick which the killer actually sits on to push it home. She knew too the importance to a novel of the heart-stopping moment when the body is discovered. In *Clutch of Constables* we share Troy's horror as she looks down at the body of Hazel Rickerby-Carrick bobbing and bumping against the starboard side of the river steamer, "idiotically bloated, her mouth drawn into an outlandish rictus grinning through discoloured foam." Death is never glamorised nor trivialised by Ngaio Marsh.

If Ngaio Marsh worked largely within the conventions of the detective novel of her age, in which way did she transcend these conventions, and transcend them so successfully that her novels are still read with pleasure while so many of her contemporaries are only named in the reference books of crime? Firstly, I suggest it lay in her power of characterisation, not only in the sensitive and attractive portrayal of Alleyn and his wife, Troy, but in the rich variety of characters who people her thirty-two novels. Her eccentrics are never caricatures. I remember particularly the president, The Boomer, in *Black as He's Painted*, poor deluded Florence Rubrick in *Died in the Wool*, Nurse Kettle in *Scales of Justice*, the distinctive Maori Rua Te Kahu in *Colour Scheme*, the Lamprey family depicted in *A Surfeit of Lampreys* with love but with insight and honesty. It is because in a Ngaio Marsh novel we can believe in the people and enter for our comfort and entertainment into a real world inhabited by credible human beings, so that some critics, including Julian Symons, have deplored her need to introduce murder, a view which occasionally she appeared to share. She wrote of her characters:

> I wish I could set them up in an orderly, well-planned fashion, as I'm sure my brothers and sisters-in-crime do. But no.

However much I try to discipline myself as to plot and general whodunnitry, I always find myself writing about a set of people in a milieu that for one reason or another attracts me, and then, bad cess to it, I have to involve them in some crime or other. Does this mean one is a straight novelist manquée?

It is indeed the set of people in a milieu which so powerfully attracts us as readers. Perhaps the most valid criticism of Ngaio Marsh is that she was too concerned with the details of the "whodunnitry." The novels have great vitality and originality while the scene is being set and the characters assembled, but tend to sag in the middle, borne down by the weight of police interrogation and routine investigation. The distinction she drew between a novel and a detective story is, of course, one which finds little favour with crime writers today; we feel entitled to be judged as novelists, not as mere fabricators of mystery. But it was a distinction reaching back to the Victorians and was a view shared by other crime writers of her time, including, somewhat surprisingly, Dorothy L. Sayers at the start of her career.

And finally, but certainly not last, there is the

quality of her writing, particularly her descriptive powers. Sometimes it is a single word which reveals her mastery. *Singing in the Shrouds* begins with a description of the London docks, and the tall cranes are described as "pontifical," an arresting and vivid image. H. R. F. Keating, who includes *A Surfeit of Lampreys* in his collection of the hundred best crime novels ever written, instances one sentence from that novel, which describes the heroine, Roberta, arriving from New Zealand by boat in London. She looks out at the other ships at anchor in the early morning light, and, Ngaio Marsh writes, "Stewards, pallid in their undervests, leant out of portholes to stare." The picture is arresting, original and certainly described from personal experience. But for me, perhaps not surprisingly, it is the New Zealand novels which include some of her best descriptive writing: her native country seen through an artist's eyes and described with a writer's voice.

Reading the best of Ngaio Marsh, I feel that there was always a dichotomy between her talent and the genre she chose. So why did she pursue it with such regularity, producing thirty-two novels in forty-eight years? They were quickly written, principally to supply a regular and sufficient income for her to live and dress well, and to enable her to continue her main interest, which was the promotion of the theatre, particularly Shakespeare's plays, in her native New Zealand. Marsh was a deeply reserved, indeed in some respects a private person, and she may well have felt that to extend the scope of her talent would be to betray aspects of her personality which she profoundly wished to remain secret. There was, too, the complication that she lived a double life. New Zealand was her birthplace and she wrote about it with affection, but her heart was in England and some of her happiest memories were when she took the long journey from the South Island to London. Her response to New Zealand was always ambivalent. She disliked and criticised the New Zealand accent, was uncertain in her literary portrayal of the Maoris, found her chief and most lasting friendship among a family of English aristocrats and retained a romantic view of the perfect English gentleman, a species to which, of course, her detective Roderick Alleyn belonged.

When Dorothy L. Sayers finished with Lord Peter and transferred her creative enthusiasm to her theological plays, she could comfort herself that she had done well with her aristocratic sleuth, and in *Gaudy Night* had used the detective story to say something about the almost sacramental importance of work and the problems for women of reconciling the claims of heart and mind which, she wrote, had been important to her all her life. Margery Allingham widened the scope of her talent so that the later novels are markedly superior to those written earlier in both characterisation and plot, while Agatha Christie knew precisely what she could do best and did it with remarkable consistency and regularity throughout a long writing life. It seems to me that only Ngaio Marsh—popular as she was and indeed remains—could have left a more impressive legacy as a novelist.

All four women had their secrets. Dorothy L. Sayers concealed the birth of her illegitimate son from her parents and close friends until her death. Her parents never knew they had a grandson. Agatha Christie never explained or spoke about her mysterious disappearance in 1926, which became a national scandal; Margery Allingham suffered much ill-health and personal anguish at the end of her life. Both Christie and Marsh falsified their ages, Marsh by actually altering her birth certificate. The secrets of their characters' lives were finally explained by the brilliance of Hercule Poirot, Albert Campion, Lord Peter or Roderick

Alleyn, but their own secrets remained inviolate until after their deaths, when all secrets, however carefully guarded or pitiable, fall prey to the insistent curiosity of the living.

Christie, Allingham and Marsh successfully continued writing detective stories well after the Second World War. Christie's last detective story, *Postern of Fate*, was published in 1973, Allingham's *Cargo of Eagles* in 1966 and Marsh's *Light Thickens* in 1982. Dorothy L. Sayers's last full-length detective story, *Busman's Honeymoon*, was first published in 1937 and reissued by Gollancz in 1972. But by the time it first appeared, Sayers was already losing interest in her aristocratic detective and turning her attention to her theological plays, and finally to her half-completed translation of Dante's *Divine Comedy*, which was to be her creative passion for the rest of her life. But no novelist can distance herself from the social and political changes of contemporary life, and those detective writers who lasted into the new age, symbolised by that mushroom cloud over Hiroshima, necessarily had to adapt their fictional worlds to less comfortable times. Agatha Christie did so with some success, but even so, when a character in her books refers to returning from the war, or his experience during the war, I have to look back to the date of publication to know whether he is referring to the Great War of 1914–18 or the 1939–45 conflict.

In the Agatha Christie novels the changes in contemporary life are mostly shown by the inconveniences suffered by the characters in obtaining servants, good service from tradesmen or maintaining their houses. Superintendent Spence, the retired policeman in *Hallowe'en Party*, published in 1969, deplores the way that girls are no longer looked after by their aunts and older sisters and that "more girls nowadays marry wrong 'uns than they ever used to in my time." Mrs. Drake complains that "mothers and families generally" were not looking after their children properly any more. There are complaints that too many people who ought to be under mental restraint are allowed to wander round freely at risk to the public and that those who went to church only got the modern version of the Bible, which had no literary merit whatsoever. Altogether things are not as they were in St. Mary Mead. Poirot, however, is little changed, although in *Hallowe'en Party* he admits to dyeing his hair. Strangely, however, he now speaks like an Englishman but still, to Mrs. Oliver's dismay, insists on wearing patent leather shoes in the country. The limp which affected him when we first encountered him has long since disappeared.

While Roderick Alleyn shows no sign of development for either good or ill, Allingham's Albert Campion becomes more serious and Lord Peter Wimsey is elevated into a wish-fulfilment hero, the kind of man his creator would obviously have liked to marry: the scholar manqué of *Gaudy Night*, standing with the Warden of All Souls outside St. Mary's Church having listened to the University sermon. But the great international changes of the immediate post-war years largely passed these writers by in their fiction, though not in their lives, as no doubt was artistically understandable. In the words of Jane Austen in *Mansfield Park*:

> Let other pens dwell on guilt and misery. I quit such odious subjects as soon as I can, impatient to restore every body, not greatly in fault themselves, to tolerable comfort, and to have done with all the rest.

Miss Marple would have approved.

6

Telling the Story: Setting, Viewpoint, People

"It is my belief, Watson, founded upon my experience, that the lowest and vilest alleys of London do not present a more dreadful record of sin than does the smiling and beautiful countryside."

Arthur Conan Doyle, "The Adventure of the Copper Beeches"

READING ANY work of fiction is a symbiotic act. We the readers contribute our imagination to that of the writer, willingly entering his world, participating in the lives of its people and forming from the author's words and images our own mental picture of people and places. The setting in any novel is therefore an important element of the whole book. Place, after all, is where the characters play out their tragicomedies, and it is only if the action is firmly rooted in a physical reality that

It was my story. A murder mystery. A who-done-it-and-got-away-with-it-until-he-wrote-about-it.

we can enter fully into their world. This is not to suggest that setting is more important than characterisation, narrative and structure; all four must be held in creative tension and the whole story written in compelling language if the book is to survive beyond its first month of publication. Many readers if questioned would opt for characterisation as the vital element in fiction, and, indeed, if the characters fail to convince, the novel is no more than a lifeless unsatisfying narrative. But the setting is where these people live, move and have their being, and we need to breathe their air, see with their eyes, walk the paths they tread and inhabit the rooms the writer has furnished for them. So important is this identification that many novels are named for the place on which the action is centred; obvious examples are *Wuthering Heights*, *Mansfield Park*, *Howards End* and *Middlemarch*, where the setting exerts a unifying and dominant influence on both the characters and the plot. I aimed to make this true of the River Thames in my novel *Original Sin*, where the river links both the more dramatic events of the story and the mood of the people who live or work near it. To one it is a source of continual fascination and pleasure, her riverside flat a symbol of ambition achieved, while to another the dark ever-flowing stream is a terrifying reminder of loneliness and death.

Some novelists in the canon of English fiction have created imaginary places in such detail and with so much care that they become real for both writer and reader. Anthony Trollope said of Framley Parsonage that he had added to the English counties, that he knew its roads and railways, its towns and parishes, and which hunts rode over it, and that there was "no name given to a fictitious site which does not represent to me a spot of which I know all the accessories, as though I had lived and wandered there." Similarly, Thomas Hardy created Wessex, of which one can draw a map, a dream county which has "by degrees, solidified into a utilitarian region which people can go to, take a house in, and write to the papers from." Writers of detective fiction seldom have space to describe a setting in such detail, but although it may be done with more economy, the place should be as real to the reader as Barchester and Wessex. I think it important too that the setting, which being integral to the whole novel, should be perceived through the mind of one of the characters, not merely described by the authorial voice, so that place and character interact and what the eye takes in influences the mood and the action.

One function of the setting is to add credibility to the story, and this is particularly important with crime fiction, which often deals with bizarre, dramatic and horrific events which need to be rooted in a place so tangible that the reader can enter it as he might a familiar room. If we believe in the place we can believe in the characters. In addition the setting can from the first chapter establish the mood of the novel, whether of suspense, terror, apprehension, menace or mystery. We have only to think of Conan Doyle's *The Hound of the Baskervilles*, of that dark and sinister mansion set in the middle of the fog-shrouded moor, to appreciate how important setting can be to the establishment of atmosphere. *The Hound of Wimbledon Common* would hardly provide such a frisson of terror.

But the setting of a detective story can emphasise the terror by contrast while, paradoxically, also providing a relief from horror. The poet W. H. Auden, for whom the reading of detective stories was an addiction, examined the genre in the light of Christian theology in his well-known essay "The Guilty Vicarage." He states:

> In the detective story, as in its mirror image, the Quest for the Grail, maps (the ritual of space) and timetables (the ritual of

time) are desirable. Nature should reflect its human inhabitants, i.e., it should be the Great Good Place; for the more Eden-like it is, the greater the contradiction of the murder. . . . The corpse must shock not only because it is a corpse but also because, even for a corpse, it is shockingly out of place, as when a dog makes a mess on a drawing-room carpet.

He believed, as I think do most British writers of the detective story, that the single body on the drawing-room floor can be more horrific than a dozen bullet-ridden bodies down Raymond Chandler's mean streets, precisely because it is indeed shockingly out of place.

I have used setting in this way to enhance danger and terror by contrast in a number of my novels. In *A Taste for Death* the two bodies, each with its head almost severed, are discovered in a church vestry by a gentle spinster and the young truant she has befriended. The contrast between the sanctity of the setting and the brutality of the murders intensifies the horror and can produce in the reader a disorientating unease, a sense that the ordained order has been overturned and we no longer stand on firm ground. In *An Unsuitable*

Job for a Woman, my first book featuring the young woman detective Cordelia Gray, a particularly appalling and callous murder takes place in high summer in Cambridge, where wide lawns, sun-dappled stone and the sparkling river recall to Cordelia's mind some words by John Bunyan: "Then I saw that there was a way to Hell, even from the gate of Heaven." It is often these paths to hell, not the destination, which provide for a crime novelist the most fascinating avenues to explore.

Detective novelists have always been fond of setting their stories in a closed society, and this has a number of obvious advantages. The stain of suspicion cannot be allowed to spread too far if each suspect is to be a rounded, credible, breathing human being, not a cardboard cut-out to be ritually knocked down in the last chapter. And in a self-contained community—hospital, school, office, publishing house, nuclear power station— where, particularly if the setting is residential, the characters often spend more time with working colleagues than they do with their families, the irritation that can emerge from such cloistered and unsought intimacy can kindle animosity, jealousy and resentment, emotions which, if they are sufficiently strong, can smoulder away and eventually explode into the destructive finality of violence. The isolated community can also be an epitome of the wider world outside and this, for a writer, can be one of the greatest attractions of the closed communal setting, particularly as the characters are being explored under the trauma of an official investigation for murder, a process which can destroy the privacies both of the living and of the dead.

The village setting has always been popular— typically, of course, in Agatha Christie—since an English village is itself a closed society and one which, whether we live in a village or not, retains a powerful hold on our imagination, an image compounded of nostalgia for a life once experienced or imagined and a vague unfocused longing to escape the city for a simpler, less frenetic and more peaceful life. It is interesting how vividly we the readers create the rural setting for ourselves, often powerfully helped by images from television or film. I don't think Agatha Christie has anywhere described in detail St. Mary Mead but we know the village street, the church, the cottage, genuinely old but untarnished by time, with its neat front garden, shining knocker and, within, Miss Marple, with her mixture of gentle authority and kindness, explaining to her latest maid that the dusting leaves something to be desired.

Settings, particularly landscapes, are often most effectively described when the writer uses a place with which he is intimately familiar. If we want to know what it is like to be a detective in twenty-first-century Edinburgh we can learn more from Ian Rankin's Rebus novels than we can from any official guidebook, as we move with Rebus down the roads and alleyways of the city and into its pubs and its public and private buildings. Ruth Rendell has used East Anglia and London, both places with which she is familiar, for some of her most admired novels written under the pseudonym Barbara Vine. East Anglia has a particular attraction for detective novelists: the remoteness of the east coast, the dangerous encroaching North Sea, the bird-loud marshes, the emptiness, the great skies, the magnificent churches and the sense of being in a place alien, mysterious and slightly sinister, where it is possible to stand under friable cliffs eaten away by the tides of centuries and imagine that we hear the bells of ancient churches buried under the sea.

Oxford has provided the setting for many detective stories by men and women who have lived or have been educated there, and who can walk with confident familiarity through its quads and down its famous streets. In the words of Edmund Crispin in his novel *The Moving Toy-shop*: "It is true that the ancient and noble city of Oxford is, of all the towns of England, the likeliest progenitor of unlikely events and persons." The air of Oxford has indeed proved peculiarly susceptible to fictional death and, although Cambridge has given us Professor Glyn Daniel's Sir Richard Cherrington, there is no competition in the murder stakes. The modern writer who comes first to mind when one thinks of Oxford is Colin Dexter, who with his Inspector Morse has ensured that, in fiction, Oxford is the most murderous city in the U.K. Dorothy L. Sayers, Oxford-educated, used the city and her imaginary women's college in *Gaudy Night*, and other detective novelists with whom we can walk these ancient and hallowed quads are Michael Innes, John C. Masterman and Margaret Yorke. Here too we have the power of contrast, a setting both beautiful and austere with which many readers will already be familiar, adding credibility to the plot while enabling them to contribute their own experience and visual images to that of the detective.

Setting in a more limited sense, particularly

architecture and houses, is important to characterisation, since people react to their environment and are influenced by it. When an author describes a room in the victim's house, perhaps the one in which the body is found, the description can tell the perceptive reader a great deal about the victim's character and interests. Furniture, books, pictures, personal articles in cupboards and on shelves, all the sad detritus of the dead life tell their story. For this reason the place in which the body is found is particularly revealing, and I regard the description of the finding of the body as one of the most important chapters of a detective novel. To find a murdered corpse is a horrible, sometimes life-changing experience for most normal people, and the writing should be vivid and realistic enough to enable the reader to share the shock and horror, the revulsion and the pity. The emotions of that moment and the language used to convey them should, in my view, reflect the person who makes the discovery. In *A Taste for Death* the description is particularly horror-invoking with the frequent reiteration of the word "blood," because that is how the gentle and kindly spinster Miss Wharton experiences the moment of discovering the two bodies with their heads almost severed. In contrast, when

Commander Adam Dalgliesh nearly stumbles over the body of a woman on a Suffolk beach his emotions are inevitably those of a professional detective. So although he is intrigued by his different emotional responses, between being called to a body knowing roughly what he will find and coming upon it unexpectedly at night on a lonely beach, nevertheless, almost instinctively, he is careful not to disturb the scene and notes all the details with the experienced eyes of an investigating officer. In Dorothy L. Sayers's first detective novel, *Whose Body?*, the corpse is found naked in the bath of a nervous and innocent architect, and the book begins with this image. The first question facing the police—and, of course, her detective Lord Peter Wimsey—is whether this was the corpse of Sir Reuben Levy, the missing Jewish financier. Whether the victim had or had not been circumcised would have answered the question at once, but this was a clue Miss Sayers was not permitted by her publishers to include in her novel, and no doubt had she done so there would have been an outcry among the respectable readers of the Golden Age.

The detective story is neither irrational nor romantic, and its clues are rooted in the reality and minutiae of everyday life. This means that

British writers who look to a foreign country for their setting need not only a sensitive response to the country's topography, speech and people, but a knowledge of its social structure, including the criminal justice system. Writers who have achieved notable success include Michael Dibdin (1947–2007), whose stories featuring the professional detective Inspector Aurelio Zen are set in Italy, a country in which he had resided. H. R. F. Keating's Indian detective, Inspector Ganesh Vinayak Ghote of the Bombay Criminal Investigation Department, first appeared in *The Perfect Murder* in 1964. Ghote is attractively human, diffident and occasionally prone to error, but shrewd and intelligent, and it is remarkable how confident was Keating's touch in describing a country which, when he brought Ghote to life, he had never visited. A comparatively recent arrival is Alexander McCall Smith's Precious Ramotswe, the proprietor of the "No. 1 Ladies' Detective Agency" in Botswana. Mma Ramotswe's heart is as ample as is her frame, and although the most atrocious murders are unlikely to come her way, any injustice, large or small, engages her energies and compassion.

All these three characters, as well as their profession, have a private domestic life in which we can participate. The detective, whether professional or amateur, needs a domestic setting if the reader is to enter fully into his life, and most writers provide for their detective a known and familiar place in which he can be at home. The name Miss Jane Marple inevitably conjures up St. Mary Mead, and although Ruth Rendell's Chief Inspector Wexford does occasionally travel outside England, we know that his natural place is Kingsmarkham in Sussex. Some detectives, of course, are more precisely housed. There can be very few aficionados of fictional murder who don't know that 221B Baker Street is the address of Sherlock Holmes, that Lord Peter Wimsey lives in an apartment at 110A Piccadilly, Albert Campion in Bottle Street and Poirot in a modern London flat distinguished by the starkness and regularity of its contemporary furniture and, we may be sure, by the total absence of dust or disarray. If details of the apartments are not given, we can provide ourselves with a lively picture of these sanctums from the television series; indeed, it is often television rather than the books themselves that furnishes us with our pictures of both the characters and the setting.

And their houses are more than a living space for the detective hero. They provide for us, the readers, reassuring safe houses of the mind from which we too can venture forth vicariously to encounter murder and danger before returning to domestic comfort and safety. Readers of Dorothy L. Sayers, travelling home to mortgaged Metroland or worried by the threat of unemployment and the storm clouds over Europe, must have entered with relief into Lord Peter's flat with the fire burning, shedding its light on the bronze chrysanthemums, the comfortable chairs and the grand piano, while Bunter deferentially offers them a glass of expensive sherry or vintage wine and Lord Peter entertains them by playing Scarlatti. Sherlock Holmes's apartment, as described by Watson, perhaps offers a more dramatic and disturbing welcome, although we can rely on Mrs. Hudson to put things to right. All Holmes's adventures start here, and it is to this sanctum that he returns, so that it becomes a safe haven for the reader who can share this assurance of safety and home comfort before setting out with Holmes and Watson on yet one more perilous adventure. Michael Innes has admitted that his hero's natural setting was a great house and that Sir John Appleby found his way into those august dwellings largely because it was the kind of life he fancied. But for his creator the mansion or great country seat was really an extension of the sealed room, with the added advantage that it could define the territorial boundaries of the mystery more effectively and interestingly than could a cramped flat or semi-detached villa.

My own detective novels, with rare exceptions, have been inspired by the place rather than by a method of murder or a character; an example is *Devices and Desires*, which had its genesis while I was on a visit of exploration in East Anglia, standing on a deserted shingle beach. There were a few wooden boats drawn up on the beach, a couple of brown nets slung between poles and drying in the wind, and, looking out over the sullen and dangerous North Sea, I could imagine myself standing in the same place hundreds of years ago with the taste of salt on my lips and the constant hiss and withdrawing rattle of the tide. Then, turning my eyes to the south, I saw the great outline of Sizewell nuclear power station and immediately I knew that I had found the setting for my next novel.

This moment of initial inspiration is always one of great excitement. I know that, however long the writing may take, I shall eventually have a novel. The idea takes possession of my mind and gradually over the months the book takes shape, the characters appear and become increasingly real to me, I know who will be murdered and where, when, how, why and by whom. I decide how my detective, Adam Dalgliesh, can logically be brought in to investigate outside the Metropolitan Police area. I began my research by visiting nuclear power stations in Suffolk and Dorset, speaking to the scientists and other staff and learning as much as I needed to know about nuclear power and the way a power station is run. As usual, all the people I consulted were unfailingly helpful. The novel which resulted from this research and the long months of writing began with that moment of solitude on an East Anglian beach.

One of the first decisions any novelist has to make, of equal importance to the choice of setting, is viewpoint. Through whose mind, eyes and ears should we, the readers, participate in the plot? Here the writer of detective stories has a particular problem arising from Monsignor Ronald Knox's insistence that the reader should not be allowed to follow the murderer's thoughts, a prohibition on which Dorothy L. Sayers so feelingly dwelt. But I wonder whether there might not be exceptions to Monsignor Knox's rule. Surely there must be some moments when the murderer's thoughts are not dominated by the enormity of what he has done and the risks of exposure. Could the writer not enter into his mind when he wakes in the small hours with memories of some traumatic event in his childhood which the writer can exploit in clue-making and use to give some idea of the killer's character? And there must be other brief moments in the day when something other than his own peril occupies his mind. But the difficulty remains.

The first-person narrative has the advantage of immediacy and of reader identification and sympathy with the one whose voice he hears. It can also be an aid to credibility, since the reader is more likely to suspend disbelief in the more improbable twists in the plot when hearing the explanation from the person most concerned. "Looking back now I cannot really explain why I decided to put my wife's body in the refuse sack, carry it with some difficulty to the boot of the car and drive a hundred and fifty miles to drop it over Beachy Head. But I was desperate to get away from the house as quickly as possible and it seemed a good idea at the time." I doubt whether this passage has ever been penned, but we have all read some uncomfortably like it. But the disadvantage of a first-person narrative is that the reader can only know what the narrator knows, seeing only through his eyes and experiencing only what he experiences and, in general, it is more appropriate to the fast-action thriller than to the detective story. One of the most effective uses of first-person narrative is by Raymond Chandler. In the brilliant opening to *The Big Sleep* the reader learns from a few short sentences where we are, what the day is like, the occupation of the hero, something about his personality, details of the clothes he is wearing, and finally why he is waiting at that particular door.

The story told by the Watson figure is less restricting because we can get his view of the detective's character and methods as well as the progress of the investigation, and was used with some success in the early days of the Golden Age. There is, however, the danger that if the character is portrayed as more than a functional necessity he will become too alive, too interesting and too important to the plot, competing as hero with the detective; if he is not vitally alive he becomes a superfluous if convenient mouthpiece for information which could be more subtly and interestingly conveyed.

Then there is the variation of the first-person narrative in which the story is told in the form of letters or in the actual voices of the characters, of which *The Moonstone* is a prime example. Dorothy L. Sayers was so admiring of Wilkie Collins's achievement that she decided to follow his example and write a novel more ambitious than her existing work and which would not feature Lord Peter Wimsey. In a letter to her scientific collaborator Eustace Barton, M.D., she wrote:

> In this story . . . it is obvious that there must be a powerful love interest, and I am going to turn my mind to making this part of the book as modern and powerful as possible. The day of the two nice young people whose chaste affection is rewarded on the final page, has rather gone by.

Apart from the wish to do something new, she said she was looking forward to getting a rest from Lord Peter because "his everlasting breeziness does become a bit of a tax at times." The novel, *The Documents in the Case*, was loosely based on the tragic Thompson–Bywaters murder, where a dull and unloved husband is killed by the young lover of his wife, and the story is told variously through letters from a young man living in the same house as the married couple, the other participants in the story, the killer, and newspaper reports giving at length the evidence from the coroner's inquests. But Sayers knew that she hadn't succeeded in her ambition. The love affair is too tawdry and uninteresting to generate the passion necessary to provoke murder, and the novel is a depressing read. Sayers herself wrote:

> In my heart I know I have made a failure of it. . . . It has produced a mingled atmosphere of dullness and gloom which will, I fear, be fatal to the book. . . . I wish I could have done better with the brilliant plot.

It was an experiment she was not to repeat. No other crime novelist as far as I know has attempted to copy let alone emulate Wilkie Collins, but it would be interesting if someone were to try.

My own choice of viewpoint is partly authorial, a detached recorder of events, and partly to move into the minds of the different characters, seeing with their eyes, expressing their emotions, hearing their words. Most often the character will be Dalgliesh, Kate Miskin or a more junior member of the detective team, one of the suspects or a witness. This for me makes a novel more complex and interesting, and can also have a note of irony as this shifting viewpoint can show how differently we can all perceive the same event. I feel it is important, however, not to alter the viewpoint in any one chapter. The distinguished critic Percy Lubbock discussed the question of viewpoint in his 1921 book *The Craft of Fiction*. The novelist, he said, can either describe the characters from outside, as an impartial or partial observer, or can assume omniscience and describe them from within, or can place himself in the position of one of them and affect to be in the dark as to the motives of the rest. What he must not do, however, is to mix his methods and change from one point of view to another—as Dickens had done in *Bleak House* and Tolstoy in *War and Peace*. But there is no rule relating to the novel which a genius can't successfully circumvent—and I generally agree with E. M. Forster, who writes in his book *Aspects of the Novel*:

So next time you read a novel do look out for the "point of view"—that is to say, the relation of the narrator to the story. Is he telling the story and describing the characters from the outside, or does he identify himself with one of the characters? Does he pretend that he knows and foresees everything? Or does he go in for being surprised? Does he shift his point of view—like Dickens in the first three chapters of *Bleak House*? And if he does, do you mind? I don't.

If we are talking of a genius, nor do I.

When I settled down in the mid-1950s to begin my first novel, it never occurred to me to make a start with anything other than a detective story. Mysteries were my favourite relaxation reading, and I felt that if I could write one successfully it would stand a good chance of acceptance by a publisher. I had no wish to write an autobiographical first novel based on my experience of childhood trauma, the war or my husband's illness, although I have come to believe that most fiction is autobiographical and some autobiography partly fiction. I have always been fascinated by structure in the novel, and detective fiction presented a number of technical problems, mainly how to construct a plot which was both credible and exciting with a setting which came alive for readers, and characters who were believable men and women faced with the trauma of a police investigation into murder. I therefore saw the detective story as an ideal apprenticeship for someone setting out with small hope of making a fortune but with ambitions to be regarded eventually as a good and serious novelist.

One of the first decisions was, of course, my choice of detective. If I started today it is likely that I would choose a woman, but this was not an option at the time when women were not active in the detective force. The main choice, therefore, was whether to have a male professional or an amateur of either sex, and as I was aiming at as much realism as possible, I chose the first option and Adam Dalgliesh, named after my English teacher at Cambridge High School, took root in my imagination.

I had learnt a lesson from Dorothy L. Sayers and Agatha Christie, both of whom started out with eccentric detectives with whom in time they became thoroughly disenchanted. So I decided to begin with a less egregiously bizarre character and ruthlessly killed off wife and newborn son in order to avoid involving myself in his emotional life, which I felt would be difficult successfully to incorporate into the structure of the classical detective story. I gave him the qualities I personally admire in either sex—intelligence, courage but not foolhardiness, sensitivity but not sentimentality, and reticence. I felt that this would provide me with a credible professional policeman capable of development should this first novel be the first of a series. A serial detective has, of course, particular advantages: an established character who does not have to be introduced afresh with each novel, a successful career in crime-solving which can add gravitas, an established family history and background and, above all, reader identification and loyalty. It is common for new hardback and paperback novels to carry the name of the detective on the jacket as well as that of the author and the title, so that prospective readers can be reassured that they will indeed encounter an old friend.

And what of the other characters, particularly the victim and the unfortunate suspects? They should certainly be more than stock figures provided out of necessity but in the Golden Age were rarely in themselves of particular interest; nothing more was required of the victim than that he or she should be an undesirable, dangerous or unpleasant person whose death need cause no grief to anyone. It is certainly not easy to make the victim sympathetic, since he must necessarily have provoked murderous hatred for diverse reasons in a small group of people and usually, once dead, could be safely carried off to the mortuary, where he was unlikely to receive the compliment of an autopsy. He has served his purpose and can be put out of mind. But if we do not care, or indeed to some extent empathise with the victim, it surely hardly matters to us whether he lives or dies. The victim is the catalyst at the heart of the novel and he dies because of who he is, what he is and where he is, and the destructive power he exercises, acknowledged or secret, over the life of at least one desperate enemy. His voice may be stilled for most of the novel, his testimony given in the voices of others, by the detritus he leaves in his rooms, his drawers and cupboards, and by the scalpels of the forensic pathologist, but for the reader, at least in thought, he must be powerfully alive. Murder is the unique crime, and its investigation tears down the privacy of both the living and the dead. It is this study of human beings under the stress of this self-revelatory probing which for a writer is one of the chief attractions of the genre.

The suspects should, I feel, be sufficient in number to provide the puzzle, and more than five is difficult if each is to be a credible living and breathing human being with motives that the reader will find convincing. And here again is the difficulty. In the Golden Age readers could accept that the victim was killed because he had damaging information about the murderer's sexual immorality, but today this will hardly suffice. People happily and lucratively confess their sexual adventures to the press with few if any detrimental consequences to career or reputation. But the fashion in public infamy changes; today the mere suggestion of paedophilia would be damaging probably beyond redemption. Money, particularly great wealth, is always a credible motive for murder, as is revenge and that deep-seated hatred which makes it almost impossible to tolerate the continued existence of an enemy. In one of my novels Dalgliesh remembers the words of a detective sergeant under whom he had served as a new recruit. "All motives can be explained under the letter L: lust, lucre, loathing and love. They'll tell you the most dangerous is loathing but don't you believe it, boy; the most dangerous is love." Certainly the desire to avenge someone deeply loved, to protect or save them, is always a credible motive and for such a murderer we may feel a measure of sympathy and self-identification. In the words of Ivy Compton-Burnett in a conversation with M. Jourdain in 1945:

I never see why murder and perversion of justice are not normal subjects for a plot, or why they are particularly Elizabethan or Victorian, as some reviewers seem to think. . . . I believe it would go ill with many of us, if we were faced with a strong temptation, and I suspect that with some of us it does go ill.

In the detective story it frequently goes very ill indeed.

When I have spoken of my craft over the past decades, one of the commonest questions the audience asks is whether I draw my characters from real life. I tended at first to say no, meaning that I have never taken people from life—members of the family, friends or colleagues—and after a few judicious alterations in appearance or character, put them in a book. But my answer was disingenuous. Of course I take my characters from real life; from where else can I take them? But the person I look to most is myself for experience endured or rejoiced in over nearly ninety years of living in this turbulent world. If I need to write about a character afflicted with such shyness that every new job, every encounter, becomes a torment, I am blessed not to suffer such misery. But I know from the embarrassments and uncertainties of adolescence what such shyness can feel like and it is my job to relive it and find the words to express it. And characters grow like plants in an author's mind during the months of writing, seeming to reveal more and more of themselves. As Anthony Trollope said in his *Autobiography*:

> They must be with him as he lies down to sleep, and as he wakes from his dreams. He must learn to hate them and to love them. . . . He must know of them whether they be cold-blooded or passionate, whether true or false, and how far true and how far false. The depth and the breadth, and the narrowness and the shallowness of each should be clear to him.

And however well I think I know my characters, they reveal themselves more clearly during the writing of the book, so that at the end, however carefully and intricately the work is plotted, I never get exactly the novel I planned. It feels, indeed, as if the characters and everything that happens to them exists in some limbo of the imagination, so that what I am doing is not inventing them but getting in touch with them and putting their story down in black and white, a process of revelation, not of creation. But the process of creation remains mysterious. One writer who has attempted to explain it is E. M. Forster. The well-known passage may be a little high-flown, a little exaggerated in the importance Forster ascribes to the subconscious, but it comes with the authority of the author of *A Passage to India*, and I think most artists, whatever their medium, feel that it gets close to at least part of the truth.

> What about the creative state? In it a man is taken out of himself. He lets down as it were a bucket into his subconscious, and draws up something which is normally beyond his reach. He mixes this thing with his normal experiences, and out of the mixture he makes a work of art. . . . And when the process is over, when the picture or symphony or lyric or novel (or whatever it is) is complete, the artist, looking back on it, will wonder how on earth he did it. And indeed he did not do it on earth. [E. M. Forster, *The Raison d'Etre of Criticism in the Arts*]

7

Critics and Aficionados: Why Some Don't Enjoy Them and Why Others Do

> In a perfect world there will be no need for detective stories: but then there will be nothing to detect. Their disappearance at this moment, however, will not bring the world any nearer to perfection. The high-minded would say that the removal of this form of relaxation would free the energies of the literate for the contemplation of real mysteries and the overcoming of real evils. I see no reason to count on that.
>
> *Erik Routley, "The Case against the Detective Story"*

DESPITE PROGNOSTICATIONS that the detective story, particularly in its classical form, is already outworn and doomed to die, it remains obstinately alive, and it is perhaps not surprising that during the decades since the Golden Age those critics not suscepti-

"This is criminal—two wrong spellings and improper use of a semicolon."

ble to its attractions have been vocal in their disparagement, complaining that the educated readers to whom detective fiction appeals—they include some illustrious names—should know better. Some of this aversion has been from readers who dislike detective fiction as others might dislike science fiction, romantic novels or stories in which the protagonist is a child. The field of fiction is rich and remarkably wide and we all have our favourite pastures.

One critic who was impervious to the charms of the genre was Edmund Wilson, who in 1945 published an influential essay entitled "Who Cares Who Killed Roger Ackroyd?" As Mr. Wilson had constantly been exposed to animated discussions on the merits of mystery writers, he enquired of aficionados what author they recommended him to try, and set out conscientiously to justify or modify his prejudice. His correspondents were almost unanimous in recommending Dorothy L. Sayers and placing her novel *The Nine Tailors* at the top of their reading list. After skipping what he described as "conversations between conventional English village characters," "boring information on campanology" and "the awful whimsical patter of Lord Peter," he reached the conclusion that *The Nine Tailors* was one of the dullest books he had encountered in any field. No doubt, thus filleted, it was.

Mr. Wilson and others of his ilk are certainly entitled to their preferences, and no efforts on the part of their friends are likely to change their minds. And much criticism still relates primarily to the Golden Age: the old argument that the story dominates over any interest in characterisation or setting and is frequently unconvincing; that the basic morality of the genre is strongly right-wing, upholding the right of the privileged against the dispossessed, in which working-class characters are little better than caricatures; and that detective fiction, so far from showing compassion to either victim or murderer, glories in a crude form of communal vengeance. In general these criticisms are so inappropriate to the majority of detective stories being written today that there is little point in refuting them. But a more interesting criticism made during the thirties still echoes in the minds of twenty-first-century critics. Its chief proponent was an influential American critic, Professor Jacques Barzun, who enjoyed detective stories but only those which, like the books of Agatha Christie, confined themselves to the pure puzzle. For him and those who agreed with him, the conventional mystery which relied on logical deduction, and in which the characters solved the plots from observed facts, had an intellectual and literary integrity which was lost if writers attempted to wade through the murky pools of abnormal psychology or to probe the psychological basis of their characters' actions and personalities. In short, these critics feared that the detective story might be getting above itself.

Somewhat surprisingly, Dorothy L. Sayers, who in *Gaudy Night* made theme and characterisation dominant over the plot, went some way to justify this view in her essay "Aristotle on Detective Fiction," published in 1946, taking the great philosopher as her authority.

> One may string together a series of characteristic speeches of the utmost finish as regards diction and thought, and yet fail to produce the true dramatic effect; but one will have much better success with a story which, however inferior in these respects, has a plot. . . . The first essential, the life and soul so to speak of the detective story, is the plot and the characters come second.

Very few detective novelists would hold this view today, or hold it so uncompromisingly. Their aim—and it is mine—is to write a good novel with the virtues those words imply, a novel which is at the same time a credible and satisfying mystery. This means that there must be a creative and reconciling correlation between plot, characterisation, setting and theme, and so far from the plot being dominant, it should arise naturally from the characters and the place.

Another ethical criticism of the detective story is that it has at its heart an appalling crime and the suffering of innocent people, and uses them to provide popular entertainment. In Sayers's novel *Gaudy Night*, Miss Barton, one of the Shrewsbury College tutors, challenges Harriet Vane about the morality of the books she writes. Surely the sufferings of innocent suspects ought to be taken seriously? To this Harriet replies that she does indeed take them seriously in real life, as must everyone. But was Miss Barton saying that anyone who had tragic experience of sex, for example, should never write an artificial drawing-room comedy? Although there was no comic side to murder, there could be a purely intellectual side to the detection. I myself would argue that it is possible to deal with the intellectual side of the detection while portraying with compassion and realism the emotional trauma of all the characters touched by this ultimate crime, whether as suspect, innocent bystander or indeed the perpetrator. In an Agatha Christie novel the crime is solved, the murderer arrested or dead, and the village returned to its customary calm and order. This does not happen in real life. Murder is a contaminating crime and no life which comes into close touch with it remains unaltered. The detective story is the novel of reason and justice, but it can affirm only the fallible justice of human beings, and the truth it celebrates can never be the whole truth any more than it is in a court of law.

The rarely heard objection to the detective novel that it might provide a real-life murderer with an idea or even a pattern for his crime surely need not be taken seriously. It has—although I think seldom—been used as a defence in real life, but hardly a valid or successful one. Apart from the fact that fictional murder is usually both more complicated and ingenious than murder in real life, it hardly provides a reliable model since the murderer is always found out. But the suggestion that detective fiction might influence those tempted to murder does raise a more interesting philosophical and moral question. Does every novelist have a moral responsibility for the possible effect of what he writes, and if so, what is this morality from which his responsibility derives? Are we not implying that there is an immutable value system, an accepted view of the universe, of our place in it, and a recognised standard of morality to which all right-minded people conform? Even if this were true—and, in our increasingly fragmented society, manifestly it is not—is it the business of the creative artist in any medium to express or promote it? And does it matter? I know that there are events about which I would find it repugnant to write, for example, the torture of a child. But how far any writer, even of popular fiction, has a duty to do more than the best of which he is capable within the law, is a question which is likely to concern more than detective novelists increasingly in our secular and morally confused age.

One of the criticisms still levelled at the detective story of the Golden Age is frequently voiced in the clever phrase "snobbery with violence," although when one considers Agatha Christie and her ilk, snobbery with a little local unpleasantness would be closer to the truth. The violence is necessarily there but it is so muted that it is sometimes difficult, reading an Agatha Christie, to remember exactly how the victim died. Parents might well complain if their adolescent son were continually reading Agatha Christie when it was time he turned to the books set for his next examination, but they would be extremely unlikely to complain that he was immured in nothing but horror and violent death. But the allegation of snobbery is reiterated, particularly with regard to the women writers of the 1930s, and what I think many people forget is that those writers were producing for an age in which social divisions were clearly understood and generally accepted since they seemed an immutable part of the natural order. And we have to remember that the detective novelists of the thirties had been bred to a standard of ethics and manners in public and private life which today might well be seen as elitist. Even so, Dorothy L. Sayers in her fiction can be seen as something of an intellectual snob, Ngaio Marsh as a social snob and Josephine Tey as a class snob in her characters' attitudes to their servants, and there are risible passages which are difficult to read without embarrassment, including the unfortunate tendency of Ngaio Marsh's suspects to say what a comfort it is to be interrogated by a gent. I wonder what they would have made of the Continental Op.

This acceptance of class distinction was not

confined to novelists. I have a number of volumes of the successful plays of the thirties, and almost without exception dramatists were writing for the middle class, about the middle class and were themselves middle class. This was, of course, decades before, on 8 May 1956, the English Stage Company produced John Osborne's iconoclastic play *Look Back in Anger*. Servants do appear in the interwar plays, but usually to provide what is seen as the necessary comic relief. Popular literature, whether detective stories or not, accepted the same division. Today the gap is between those who have wealth and celebrity—whether achieved through natural talent or, more commonly, as artefacts of the media—and those who have not. It is ostentatious wealth that bestows distinction and privilege. Although this new division has its disagreeable aspect, perhaps it is a fairer system since everyone can hope, however unreasonably, to win the lottery and move into the charmed circle of unlimited consumption and media attention, whereas distinction by breeding is immutably fixed at birth and intellectual ability in all classes largely the result of inherited intelligence which in the more fortunate can be fostered by good education. Snobbery is always with us; it merely embodies different prejudices and is directed at different victims. But I would expect even the most assiduous class warrior to welcome a form of popular literature which confirms the universal truth that jealousy, hatred and revenge can find a place in every human heart. In detective fiction the successful middle-class character is more often than not the murderer, and some would say with much less excuse than have the unfortunate and deprived. In general, the butler didn't do it.

The resilience of detective fiction, and particularly the fact that so many distinguished and powerful people are apparently under its spell, has puzzled both its admirers and its detractors and spawned a number of notable critical studies which attempt to explain this puzzling phenomenon. In "The Guilty Vicarage," W. H. Auden wrote that his reading of detective stories was an addiction, the symptoms being the intensity of his craving, the specificity of the story, which, for him, had to be set in rural England, and last, its immediacy. He forgot the story as soon as he had finished the book and had no wish to read it again. Should he begin a detective story and then discover it was one he had already read, he was unable to continue. In all this the distinguished poet differed from me and, I suspect, from many other lovers of the genre. I enjoy rereading my favourite mysteries although I know full well how the book will end, and although I can understand the attraction of a rural setting, I am frequently happy to venture with my favourite detectives onto unfamiliar territory.

Auden states that the most curious fact about the detective story is that it appeals precisely to people who are immune to other forms of what he describes as daydream literature. He suspects that the typical reader of detective stories is, like himself, a person who suffers from a sense of sin, by which he is not implying that mysteries are read solely by law-abiding citizens so that they may gratify vicariously the impulse to violence. The fantasy which the mystery provides is one of escape to a prelapsarian state of innocence, and the driving force behind the daydream is the discomfort of an unrecognised guilt. Since a sense of guilt seems natural to humanity, Auden's theory is not unreasonable and some critics have suggested that it explains the otherwise curious fact that the detective story had its beginning and flourishes best in Protestant countries, where the majority of people don't resort to confession to a priest in order to receive absolution. It would be interesting to test this theory, but I hardly feel that an approach to the Archbishop of Canterbury and the Cardinal Archbishop of Westminster suggesting that their priests should take an exit poll after Sunday morning services would be sympathetically received. But certainly a sense of guilt, however ungrounded, seems inseparable from our Judeo-Christian inheritance, and few people opening their door to two grave-faced detectives with a request that they should accompany them to the police station would do so without a qualm of unease, however certain they may be of their complete innocence.

Other critics, particularly it seems in the U.S.A. and Germany, have attempted to explain addiction to the genre in Freudian terms. Apparently we mystery fans are innocent in the eyes of the criminal law but are burdened with "an unconscious hysteric-passive tension," stemming in men from the "negative" Oedipus complex, in women from the "positive" Oedipus, and can obtain from detective stories temporary and vicarious release of tension. I suppose we must be grateful that, despite the complications of our psyche, we are law-abiding citizens who do no harm to others.

For those of us uneducated in the recesses of abnormal psychology, the attractions of the detective story are more obvious. Firstly, there is, of course, the story.

> Yes—oh dear yes—the novel tells a story. That is the fundamental aspect without which it could not exist. . . . We are all like Scheherazade's husband in that we want to know what happens next. That is universal and that is why the backbone of a novel has to be a story. . . . Qua story, it can have only one merit: that of making the audience want to know what happens next. And conversely it can only have one fault: that of making the audience not want to know what happens next. These are the only two criticisms that can be made on the story that is a story. It is both the lowest and simplest of literary organisms. Yet it is the highest factor common to all the very complicated organisms known as novels. [E. M. Forster, *Aspects of the Novel*]

Certainly all the major novelists in the canon of English literature have told stories, some exciting, some tragic, some slight, some mysterious, but all of them have the virtue of leaving us with a need to know what happens next as we turn each page. For a time in the late twentieth century it seemed that the story was losing its status and that psychological analysis, a complicated and occasionally inaccessible style and an egotistic introspection were taking over from action. Happily there now seems to be a return to the art of storytelling. But this, of course, the detective novel has never lost. We are presented with a mystery at the heart of the novel and we know that by the end it will be solved. Very few readers can put down a detective story until it is solved, although some have fallen into the reprehensible expedient of taking a quick look at the last chapter.

Part of the attraction of the story is this satisfaction in solving the mystery. The importance of this differs with the individual reader. Some follow the clues assiduously and at the end feel the same small triumph that they do after a successful game of chess. Others find more interest in the characterisation, the setting, the writing or the theme. Certainly if the mystery were dominant no one would wish to reread old favourites, and many of us find that, reading in bed, the comfort and reassurance of a beloved mystery is the pleasantest prelude to falling asleep. And without wading too deeply into the pools of psychological analysis, there can be no doubt that the detective story produces a reassuring relief from the tensions and responsibilities of daily life; it is particularly popular in times of unrest, anxiety and uncertainty, when society can be faced with problems which no money, political theories or good intentions seem able to solve or alleviate. And here in the detective story we have a problem at the heart of the novel, and one which is solved, not by luck or divine intervention, but by human ingenuity, human intelligence and human courage. It confirms our hope that, despite some evidence to the contrary, we live in a beneficent and moral universe in which problems can be solved by rational means and peace and order restored from communal or personal disruption and chaos. And if it is true, as the evidence suggests, that the detective story flourishes best in the most difficult of times, we may well be at the beginning of a new Golden Age.

8

Today and a Glimpse of Tomorrow

The detective novel . . . is aimed above all at the intelligence; and this could constitute for it a title to nobility. It is in any case perhaps one of the reasons for the favour it enjoys. A good detective story possesses certain qualities of harmony, internal organisation and balance, which respond to certain needs of the spirit, needs which some modern literature, priding itself on being superior, very often neglects.

Régis Messac, Le "detective novel" et l'influence de la pensée scientifique *(1929)*

THE CLASSICAL detective story is the most paradoxical of the popular literary forms. The story has at its heart the crime of murder, often in its most horrific and violent form, yet we read the novels primarily for entertainment, a comforting, even cosy relief from the anxieties, problems and irritations of everyday life. Its prime concern—indeed its

*"Did Esme Draycott really go to her lover that night?
Is Selwyn Plunkett dead or alive and well in Peru?
Was Melanie Frayle asleep or drugged? Who was
the man in the green Lagonda? Stay with us
for Part Two, after the break."*

raison d'être—is the establishment of truth, yet it employs and glories in deceit: the murderer attempts to deceive the detective; the writer sets out to deceive the reader, to make him believe that the guilty are innocent, the innocent guilty; and the better the deception the more effective the book. The detective story is concerned with great absolutes—death, retribution, punishment—yet in its clue-making it employs as the instruments of that justice the trivial artefacts and incidents of everyday life. It affirms the primacy of established law and order, yet its attitude to the police and the agencies of that law has often been ambiguous, the brilliance of the amateur detective contrasted with dull official orthodoxy and unimaginative incompetence. The detective story deals with the most dramatic and tragic manifestations of man's nature and the ultimate disruption of murder, yet the form itself is orderly, controlled, formulaic, providing a secure structure within which the imaginations of writer and reader alike can confront the unthinkable.

This paradox, true of the books of the Golden Age, remains true today, although perhaps to a lesser extent. But the detective story has changed since, as a teenager, I saved my pocket-money to buy the new book by Dorothy L. Sayers or Margery Allingham. It could hardly be otherwise. That was over seventy years ago, decades which have seen the Second World War, the atomic bomb, major advances in science and technology which have outstripped our ability to control them, great movements of a world population which threatens our resources of food and water, international terrorism and a planet at risk of becoming uninhabitable. Beside these momentous changes, no human activity, even popular art in any medium, can remain unaffected.

The way in which the typescript is physically produced has also changed dramatically. My secretary, Joyce McLennan, has been typing my novels for thirty-three years and recently we have been reminiscing about those early days when she used a manual typewriter, worked at home because she had young children, and I dictated onto a tape which her husband collected on his way home from work. She reminds me that since I also was working, the tape was often concealed in a large china pig hidden by the side gate. We then advanced to an electric typewriter, and then to a word processor, which seemed the acme of scientific progress. I still like to write by hand, but now I dictate each chapter to Joyce, who puts it onto the computer, printing it out in sections for me to revise. Finally it is sent simultaneously to my publisher, agent and editor through cyber-space, a system which I can neither operate nor understand. Many of my friends—perhaps the majority—have for years produced their books directly on the computer, but no machine made by man is user-friendly to me.

Publishing methods have also changed. New technology means that books can now be produced very quickly to meet demand. Small independent booksellers are finding it more and more difficult to compete with Internet selling. The advent and increasing popularity of the e-book has brought a dramatic change. For those of us who love books—the smell of the paper, the design, the print and the type, the feel of the book as we take it down from the shelf—reading by machine seems an odd preference. But if we accept that what is important is the text, not the means by which it comes to the reader's eyes and brain, it is easier to understand the popularity of this new resource, particularly for a generation which has become accustomed to technology from childhood. But how far, if at all, these changes will actually affect the variety and type of fiction produced remains to be seen.

What is surprising is not that the detective story has altered but that it has survived, and that what we have seen since the interwar years has been a development, not a rejection, followed by renewal. Crime fiction today is more realistic in its treatment of murder, more aware of scientific advances in the detection of crime, more sensitive to the environment in which it is set, more sexually explicit and closer than it has ever been to mainstream fiction. The difference between the crime novel in all its variety and detective fiction has become increasingly fudged, but there still remains a clear division between the generality of crime novels and the conventional detective story, even at its most exciting, which continues to be concerned with each individual death and the solving of the mystery through patient intelligence rather than physical violence and prowess.

I find it interesting that the detective hero, originated by Conan Doyle, has survived and is still at the heart of the story, like a secular priest expert in the extraction of confession, whose final revelation of the truth confers a vicarious absolution on all but the guilty. But, not surprisingly, he has changed. Because of the growing importance of realism for writers and readers, in part arising from the comparative reality of television series, the professional detective has largely taken over

from the amateur. What we have are realistic por-
trayals of human beings undertaking a difficult,
sometimes dangerous, and often disagreeable job,
beset with the anxieties common to humanity:
professional jealousies, uncooperative colleagues,
the burden of bureaucracy and difficulties with
wives or children. An example of the successful professional detective at peace with his job
is Ruth Rendell's Inspector Reginald Wexford,
who, so far from being a disillusioned maverick,
is a hard-working, conscientious, liberal-minded
police officer, happily married to Dora, who provides for him that stable background which helps
to buttress him against the worst traumas of his
daily work.

And policing itself has changed dramatically.
In the Golden Age, police forces were not yet
integrated into the forty-two large forces of today,
and major cities and their county were separately
policed. This gave opportunities for productive
rivalry as each strove to be the more efficient,
but the separation was economically expensive
and could cause difficulties in co-operation and
communication. Chief constables, so far from
coming up through the ranks, were usually retired colonels or brigadiers, experienced in leading men and promoting loyalty to a common
purpose but occasionally over-authoritative, and

representative of only one class. But they were able to know individual officers and were known by them, and both they and the policemen on the beat were familiar and reassuring figures to the much smaller and homogenous community they served. The job of policing our multicultural, overcrowded island and its stressed democracy is fundamentally different from the job in, for example, the twenties and thirties. I remember as an eight-year-old being told by my father that if ever I were alone and afraid or in difficulties I should find a policeman. Police officers are as ready to help a child in distress now as they were then, but I wonder how many parents in the more deprived inner-city areas would give that advice today. The crime novelist today needs to understand something of the ethos, ramifications and problems of this rapidly changing world, particularly if his detective is a police officer.

The Watson in the form of a sidekick, created to be less intelligent than the hero and to ask questions which the average reader might wish to put, has long since bowed out and, on the whole, to general relief. But the detective, whether professional or amateur, does need some character in whom he can rationally confide if the reader is to be provided with enough information to be engaged in the solution. For a professional detective it is usually the detective sergeant, whose background and personality provide a contrast to that of the hero and an ongoing relationship which is not always easy. The reader becomes involved in the sergeant's different domestic background and different view of the job itself. Notable examples are Colin Dexter's Morse and Lewis, Reginald Hill's Dalziel and Pascoe, Ruth Rendell's Wexford and Burden, and Ian Rankin's Rebus and Siobhan Clarke, where we have the added advantage of a woman's point of view. In the hands of such masters of the detective story they are subordinate to their boss in rank but not in importance. It is not surprising that Morse has been successfully replaced by Lewis, who has grown in authority since his promotion and now has a very different, more intellectual subordinate of his own, Sergeant Hathaway, to fulfil the function that was previously his.

A. A. Milne had a passion for detective stories, although he didn't persist in writing them, and is best known for *The Red House Mystery*, first published in 1922. In a reissue of the novel in 1926, he wrote an entertaining introduction in which he addressed the issue of the Watson.

> Are we to have a Watson? We are. Death to the author who keeps his unravelling for

the last chapter, making all the other chapters but prologue to a five-minute drama. This is no way to write a story. Let us know from chapter to chapter what the detective is thinking. For this he must watsonize or soliloquize; the one is merely a dialogue form of the other, and, by that, more readable. A Watson, then, but not of necessity a fool of a Watson. A little slow, let him be, as so many of us are, but friendly, human, likeable . . .

"Friendly, human, likeable," an accurate description of the Detective Sergeant Watsons of today, and long may they flourish.

Writers of the Golden Age, and indeed for some decades after, were little concerned with forensic or scientific research. The present system of forensic science laboratories was not yet in prospect and few of the victims were subjected to an autopsy, or if they were, this unpleasant procedure was seldom mentioned. Occasionally a post-mortem was undertaken by the local general practitioner, who within hours was able to inform the detective from exactly which poison the victim died, a feat which would occupy a modern laboratory for some weeks.

The discovery of DNA is only one, but among the most important, of the scientific and technological discoveries which have revolutionised the investigation of crime. These include advanced systems of communication, the scientific analysis of trace elements, greater definition in the analysis of blood, increasingly sophisticated cameras which can identify bloodstains among multi-stained coloured surfaces, laser techniques which can raise fingerprints from skin and other surfaces which previously offered no hope of a successful print, and medical advances which affect the work of forensic pathologists. Modern writers of detective fiction need to be methodical in their research and the results integrated into the narrative, but not so intrusively that the reader is aware of the trouble taken and feels that he is being subjected to a brief lesson in forensic science. Some novelists manage so well without the inclusion of this scientific knowledge that the reader doesn't feel the lack of it. I can remember only one instance in which Morse mentions a forensic science laboratory but, reading the books or watching the televised adaptations, we never for a moment suppose that the Thames Valley Constabulary is bereft of this necessary resource.

I like to do my own research, as do most detective novelists, and am grateful for the help I have received over the years both from the Metropolitan Police and from the scientists at the Lambeth Laboratory. But there have been mistakes. These usually arise, not from facts about which I am ignorant, but from those which I fondly and mistakenly imagine I already know. In one of my early novels I described a motorcyclist, disguised by his oilskins and goggles, "reversing noisily down the lane." This led to a letter from a male reader complaining that, although I was usually meticulous in my choice of words, the sentence gave the impression that I thought that a two-stroke motorcycle could go backwards. So indeed I did. This mistake proved expensive, leading over the years to much correspondence, invariably from male readers, sometimes explaining in minute detail and occasionally with the aid of a diagram precisely why I was wrong. Salvation came some years ago in the form of a message on a postcard which said simply, "That motorbike— it can if it's a Harley-Davidson."

The search for a new location and fresh ideas continues. Despite the reasonable view of some critics that the detective story can't exist until a society has developed an institutional system of law enforcement, a number of writers have with success looked to the past for inspiration. Private murder, as opposed to mass killing by the state, has been regarded as the unique crime in almost every society however primitive, an abomination to be avenged, if not by a legal system, by the family, involving the further shedding of blood, by banishment or public dishonour. The classical detective story can work in any age provided murder is regarded as an act which necessitates the discovery of the perpetrator and the cleansing of society of its stain. Writers who have returned to Victorian England include Peter Lovesey, with Sergeant Cribb and Constable Thackeray, and Anne Perry, whose novels feature Police Inspector Thomas Pitt and his wife, Charlotte, who assists him. Ellis Peters has written twenty novels which feature Brother Cadfael, a twelfth-century Benedictine monk, while Lindsey Davis goes back even further with her detective, Marcus Didius Falco, a private eye in ancient Rome. A notable comparative newcomer to the historical mystery is C. J. Sansom, who has become one of the most popular and accomplished crime writers. His novels are set in Tudor England, an age as dangerous as our own, particularly for those in the orbit of the formidable Henry VIII. His hero is a hunchback lawyer, Matthew Shardlake, sensitive, liberal, highly intelligent, whose life and the age of which he is part become so real that the sights, the voices, the very smell of Tudor England seem to rise from the page. The historical detective story is one of the most difficult to write well, requiring sensitive identification with the past, the ability to bring it vividly to life and meticulous research, but in expert hands it shows no sign of losing its popularity.

From the beginning, film and crime writing have enjoyed a sustaining and lucrative partnership in crime, but never more so than today. Some of the earliest films were taken from crime stories, and any list of the most memorable and successful ever made will include crime movies. In general producers have opted for the fast-action thriller with its dominant testosterone-fuelled hero and its opportunities for spectacular action sequences, stunts and a far-ranging variety of locations which modern cameramen can exploit in pictures of breathtaking natural scenery or the cluttered danger and excitement of the great cities of the world. Alfred Hitchcock, who found his inspiration in murder and mayhem, explained in a television interview the problem of filming the classical detective story. He wanted his audience to be in thrall to suspense and horror; in a detective story they were more likely to be exercising their brains in deciding who would prove to be guilty. In the end this would be revealed, and in an anticlimax rather than a final shudder. The exceptions to this dominance of the thriller in films and television are, of course, the ubiquitous Holmes and Poirot. Holmes first appeared in 1903 in an extraordinarily short silent film, *Sherlock Holmes Baffled*, and later there was a series of his adventures in two-reelers made in Denmark from 1908 to 1911. Poirot first appeared in 1931, five years after *The Murder of Roger Ackroyd* was published. It was filmed in England, and thereafter every few years Agatha Christie's iconic character has appeared in film and television played by a variety of actors, one of the most famous films being *Murder on the Orient Express* in 1974, with its international all-star cast, a story which, despite having so many improbabilities as suspects, remains a masterpiece of its type.

The classical detective story appears on television chiefly as a serial which exploits the existing popularity in print of the detective, of which Colin Dexter's Inspector Morse is probably the best known. Films and television series which, while generally adhering to the classical form of the detective story, combine clues with action are the highly successful police procedurals. The police service has provided material for film and television for decades and there has been a remarkable transition from the avuncular goodnight salute of Dixon of Dock Green, both in the film *The Blue Lamp* and on television, through the greater realism of *Z Cars*; *Softly, Softly*; *The Sweeney* to *Law and Order*. In *Prime Suspect*, written by Lynda La Plante, we are taken into the disturbing search for a psychopathic killer; the heroine, Jane Tennison, is at once an effective senior detective and a vulnerable woman coping with the cost to her emotional life of this dangerous and still predominantly masculine world. Undoubtedly the importance of film and television will increase now that DVDs enable the best to be viewed at home. But how far the demands of film and television will influence the writing of crime fiction, including the detective story, is less easy to assess.

The crime novel, including the detective story, is now international, the most distinguished both in English and foreign languages being best-sellers throughout the world, and undoubtedly the translation of detective stories into English will continue. A catalogue I picked up in a Cambridge bookshop named 730 recent and forthcoming crime novels, many of which are detective stories, and what to me is new and interesting is the number of translations. The majority are from the Swedish, but France, Poland, Italy, Russia, Iceland and Japan are represented. I can't imagine a catalogue in my youth featuring so many crime books in such variety or with so many translations from writers worldwide. The Swedish writer Henning Mankell is likely to become increasingly popular since his detective Kurt Wallander has recently successfully appeared on British television, the hero played by Kenneth Branagh. The list confirms my impression that although private sleuths still appear and in great variety, there is a growing preference among writers for a professional detective. But are we in danger of reducing the fictional police officer to a stereotype—solitary, divorced, hard-drinking, psychologically flawed and disillusioned? Real-life senior detectives are not stereotypes. Would anyone, I wonder, create a fictional detective who enjoys his work, gets on well with his colleagues, is happily married, has a couple of attractive, well-behaved children who cause him no trouble, reads the lesson in his parish church and spends his few free hours playing the cello in an amateur string quartet? I doubt whether readers would find him wholly credible, but he would certainly be an original.

Among foreign detective writers, Georges Simenon, one of the most highly regarded and influential of twentieth-century crime novelists, has been available in English for decades. We look to Simenon for a strong narrative, a setting which is brilliantly and sensitively evoked, a cast in which every character, however minor, is uniquely alive, psychological acuity and an empathy with the secret lives of apparently ordinary men and women in a style which combines economy of words with strength and elegance, and which has given him a literary reputation rare among crime novelists. Inevitably, despite the apparent simplicity of style, he is a novelist who loses much in translation, but he still exerts an influence over the modern detective story.

I was interested also in a number of Golden Age writers who are reappearing in print, published largely by small independent houses. These include such popular stalwarts as Gladys Mitchell, Nicholas Blake, H. C. Bailey and John Dickson Carr, master of the locked-room mystery. It is highly unlikely that these emotionally unthreatening and nostalgic detective stories would be written today except as ingenious and clever pastiche or as tributes to the Golden Age. How strongly the typical mysteries of the inter-war years linger in memory; invariably set in large country houses in the depths of winter, cut off from the outside world by snowdrifts and fallen telegraph wires and with a most unpleasant house guest found in the library with an ornate dagger in the heart. How fortunate that the world's greatest detective should have run his coupé into a snowdrift and taken refuge in Mayhem Manor. But does the success of a pastiche or the reissue of old favourites mean that readers for whom the detective story is primarily entertainment will begin to turn from the gritty realities of today in search of remembered satisfactions? This seems to me unlikely. I see the detective story becoming more firmly rooted in the reality and the uncertainties of the twenty-first century, while still providing that central certainty that even the most intractable problems will in the end be subject to reason.

Whether we live in a more violent age than did, for example, the Victorians is a question for statisticians and sociologists, but we certainly feel more threatened by crime and disorder than at any other time I remember in my long life. This constant awareness of the dark undercurrents of society and of human personality is probably partly due to the modern media, when details of the most atrocious murders, of civil strife and violent protests, come daily into our living rooms from television screens and other forms of modern technology. Increasingly writers of crime novels and detective stories will reflect this tumultuous world in their work and deal with it with far greater realism than would have been possible in the Golden Age. The solving of the mystery is still at the heart of a detective story but today it is no longer isolated from contemporary society. We know that the police are not invariably more virtuous and honest than the society from which they are recruited, and that corruption can stalk the corridors of power and lie at the very heart of government and the criminal justice system.

Today there is undoubtedly an increased interest in detective fiction. New novels are being reviewed with respect, many of them by names unfamiliar to me. It is apparent that publishers and readers are continuing to look for well-written mysteries which afford the expected satisfaction of a credible plot but can legitimately be enjoyed as serious novels. A number of novelists have successfully moved between detective fiction, non-fiction and mainstream novels: Frances Fyfield, Ruth Rendell writing as Barbara Vine, Susan Hill, Joan Smith, John Banville and Kate Atkinson being examples. Although I have mentioned the names of crime writers, alive and dead, to illustrate my text, I have neither the wish nor the competence to undertake the function of a reviewer. All lovers of detective fiction will have their favourites. But the variety and quality of detective fiction being produced today, both by established writers and by newcomers, will ensure that the future of the genre is in safe hands.

Our planet has always been a dangerous, violent and mysterious habitation for humankind and we all are adept at creating those pleasures and comforts, large and small, sometimes dangerous and destructive, which offer at least temporary relief from the inevitable tensions and anxieties of contemporary life. A love of detective fiction is certainly among the least harmful. We do not expect popular literature to be great literature, but fiction which provides excitement, mystery and humour also ministers to essential human needs. We can honour and celebrate the genius which produced *Middlemarch*, *War and Peace* and *Ulysses* without devaluing *Treasure Island*, *The Moonstone* and *The Inimitable Jeeves*. The detective story at its best can stand in such company, and its popularity suggests that in the twenty-first century, as in the past, many of us will continue to turn for relief, entertainment and mild intellectual challenge to these unpretentious celebrations of reason and order in our increasingly complex and disorderly world.

Bibliography and Suggested Reading

Barnard, Robert. *A Talent to Deceive: An Appreciation of Agatha Christie*. Collins, London, 1980.

Booth, Martin. *The Doctor, the Detective and Arthur Conan Doyle*. Hodder & Stoughton, London, 1997.

Craig, Patricia, and Mary Cadogan. *The Lady Investigates: Women Detectives and Spies in Fiction*. Victor Gollancz, London, 1981.

Keating, H. R. F., ed. *Crime Writers: Reflection on Crime Fiction*. BBC, London, 1978.

Lewis, Margaret. *Ngaio Marsh: A Life*. Chatto & Windus, London, 1991; The Hogarth Press, London, 1992.

Morgan, Janet. *Agatha Christie: A Biography*. Collins, London, 1984.

Most, Glenn W., and William W. Stowe, eds. *The Poetics of Murder: Detective Fiction and Literary Theory*. Harcourt Brace Jovanovich, San Diego, 1983.

Penzler, Otto, ed. *The Great Detectives*. Little, Brown, Boston and Toronto, 1978.

Reynolds, Barbara. *Dorothy L. Sayers: Her Life and Soul*. Hodder & Stoughton, London, 1993.

Reynolds, Barbara, ed. *The Letters of Dorothy L. Sayers,*

1899–1936: The Making of a Detective Novelist. Hodder
& Stoughton, London, 1995.

Stewart, R. F. *And Always a Detective: Chapters on the History of Detective Fiction.* David & Charles, Newton
Abbot, 1980.

Summerscale, Kate. *The Suspicions of Mr. Whicher or The
Murder at Road Hill House.* Bloomsbury, London, 2008.

Symons, Julian. *Bloody Murder.* Faber & Faber, London,
1972; Viking, New York, 1985; Mysterious Press, New
York, 1992.

Thompson, Laura. *Agatha Christie: An English Mystery.*
Headline Review, London, 2007.

Thorogood, Julia. *Margery Allingham: A Biography.* William
Heinemann, London, 1991. Now reissued as Julia Jones,
The Adventures of Margery Allingham. Golden Duck
Publishing, Chelmsford, 2009.

Watson, Colin. *Snobbery with Violence.* Eyre & Spottiswoode, London, 1971; Eyre Methuen, London, 1979,
1987.

Winks, Robin. *Detective Fiction.* Prentice-Hall, New Jersey,
1980.